The Asia Investor

Charting a Course Through Asia's Emerging Markets

The Asia Investor

Charting a Course Through Asia's Emerging Markets

Aaron Chaze

WILEY

John Wiley & Sons (Asia) Pte. Ltd.

Other Wiley Editorial Offices

John Wiley & Sons, 111 River Street, Hoboken, NJ 07030, USA
John Wiley & Sons, The Atrium, Southern Gate, Chichester, West Sussex, P019
    8SQ, United Kingdom
John Wiley & Sons (Canada) Ltd., 5353 Dundas Street West, Suite 400,
    Toronto, Ontario, M9B 6HB, Canada
John Wiley & Sons Australia Ltd., 42 McDougall Street, Milton, Queensland
    4064, Australia
Wiley-VCH, Boschstrasse 12, D-69469 Weinheim, Germany

Library of Congress Cataloging-in-Publication Data

ISBN 978-0470-82529-7

Typeset in 11.5/14pt Bembo by Macmillan
Printed in Singapore by Saik Wah Press Pte. Ltd.

10 9 8 7 6 5 4 3 2 1

In memory of my grandmother,
Linda Rodrigues.

Contents

Introduction   ix

Chapter 1   Asia Rising: Emerging Themes and Trends   1
Chapter 2   The Changing Investment Canvas   33
Chapter 3   Asia's Infrastructure Build-Out: The Next
             Great Investment Opportunity   71
Chapter 4   Building Brands but Keeping an Eye on
             Traditional Strengths   95
Chapter 5   Asia: The Next Great Financial Supermarket   117
Chapter 6   The Economics and Politics of Energy   129
Chapter 7   Political Stability: Asia's New Investment
             Catalyst   151

Select Bibliography   169

Index   171

Introduction

Emerging Asia was the fairytale story to surface from the economic horror that enfolded much of the world in 2008 and 2009. Right through the slump and the nascent recovery of late 2009 and early 2010, Asian markets regularly made the headlines for extraordinary macro growth numbers or spikes in the stock index. More than the numbers, though, it was the swift response of these economies to government stimulus measures that was interesting to see. But the question frequently asked is whether Asian countries, especially China, will be able to sustain the pace of growth or whether their economies will collapse under their own weight, especially if the underlying drivers turn out to be more speculative than fundamental. The question is not how sustainable is the growth (for growth rates will inevitably slow) but whether these economies have what it takes to move away from an export-led, external-trade-dominated economic philosophy and truly embrace a free-market philosophy. The focus should be on whether these countries can develop their domestic economies. The answer is linked to whether or not they are able to open their markets to domestic and foreign competition and whether they can go beyond manufacturing and enjoy a service-sector-led boom that pulls the tens of millions of unemployed or underemployed people into the mainstream economy.

Asia is buoyed by several trends that drive the opportunity across the region. These trends morphed into themes, the analysis of which forms the basis of this book. I have dwelt both on short-term factors that can be observed and tested today and on the longer-term themes that can be tested further down the road. In most cases, these powerful investment themes are shaped by events that affected Asian nations individually or collectively over the past decade and a half and thus have become deep-rooted.

The key crisis for Asia was the currency and debt crisis of 1997–98, which triggered changes in economic policies, systems, governance structures, and corporate strategies. The change has manifested itself in different ways: how Thai real-estate companies have redefined their operations; the emergence of Indian multinationals; the real evolution of regional trade in financial services; the emergence of a regional debt market; the evolution of a framework for Asian multilateral cooperation and the growing institutionalization of Asia; increased cross-border trade; a move up the value chain by commodity-dependent nations; and a move to diversify risk by commodity-surplus nations.

China and India are the oft-cited examples of Asian growth prospects but equally exciting are the emerging trends in Indonesia, Malaysia, and Vietnam. Riding these varied trends, too, are the older Asian tigers— Korea, Singapore, and Taiwan. There are also developments under way in once-stodgy Middle Eastern countries: the next decade or two could see their transformation into dynamic services-driven economies to rival Israel's current status as the region's only dynamic economy.

A number of companies are discussed in the book and are, for the most part, used for illustrative purposes only. The fact that they are mentioned should not be taken to mean that they are investment recommendations. In fact, some readers may recognize that a few of the corporate names discussed are not investment-worthy, for a variety of reasons. I have not made the distinction between investment grade and non-investment grade names since all the companies mentioned help in uncovering the investment canvas or are useful for understanding unfolding trends in an industry. What the book is intended to do, however, is to provide a framework for analyzing the investment opportunity across the region and to help readers pick their own winners.

Chapter 1

Asia Rising: Emerging Themes and Trends

During the early years of the fifteenth century, the legendary Chinese admiral and navigator Zheng He led large armadas on voyages to the far reaches of Asia, eventually crossing the vast expanse of the Indian Ocean to reach the shores of Mogadishu in East Africa. These voyages—sometimes involving fleets of up to 300 ships—were an attempt by the prosperous and progressive Ming Dynasty to spread its influence in Asia and demonstrate its growing power. More than conquest, these voyages were meant to show off the tremendous achievements of the Chinese people. This age of Chinese expansion, however, was brief, lasting for only around three decades. The natural instinct to withdraw within the confines of its borders and its cultural embrace of modesty was too strong to resist, despite the tremendous domestic and international impact of a growing, prosperous, and increasingly powerful China. To compound the philosophical and cultural tendency to introvert, the Chinese expression of power came at a time of European renaissance and renewal that led to a European golden age that resulted in the colonization, subjugation, and eventual decline of China, India, and other Asian civilizations.

Well before the economic and political growth in the Ming Dynasty, though, China had already emerged as a world trading powerhouse during the Tang Dynasty (618–907 AD), with merchant ships trading at ports in India, Sri Lanka, Persia, and Mesopotamia (modern day Iraq), and in Egypt, Ethiopia, and Somalia in North and East Africa. Chinese trade with kingdoms in India was recorded as far back as 2,000 years ago.

Economists and historians have estimated that toward the middle of the second millennium, between one-quarter and one-third of total global output came from China and India. Interestingly enough, by the 1890s China's share of global trade had fallen to just 1.5 percent, while India's had declined to 3 percent. By 1920, India's share had picked up to 4 percent, while China's had increased to just 1.9 percent. But China has had the industrial, financial, and human capital to be a dominant economic story from antiquity right up to the modern age. Like India, it has fascinated the West for a long time given its wealth and manufacturing ability. However, it was China's huge population (numbering over 300 million a hundred years ago) that emerged as a key driving force for Western traders (or factors, as they were known) to set up trading establishments or "factories" in China in the late nineteenth century. Economic writers who chronicled the early age of Western engagement with China (in the eighteenth and nineteenth centuries) pointed out that the only barrier to trade with China was the Chinese themselves. They were so conservative, introverted, and content with their own domestic production that they saw no point in trading with the West.

In the current era, the rapid recent growth and development of China is a miracle, even by its own historical standards. The story of this economic miracle that has unfolded over the past three to four decades has been well documented but merits a retelling since it has become a symbol of how a nation can collectively amplify its strengths and overcome its weaknesses while creating endless possibilities for its people. And as economic momentum swings eastward, Chinese naval vessels are once again reaching out to Asian, African, and European shores and beyond, as China projects its growing political clout at a time of tremendous economic prosperity. With all the evidence before us it would not be far-fetched to say that we are likely witnessing a resurgent Asia, with China at its head.

China's path to economic growth commenced roughly a decade before the visionary reformist leader Deng Xiaoping began to formally push his country toward a more liberal economic agenda in 1978. As Figure 1.1 illustrates, China's growth rate over the past few decades has been by no means linear, with growth trends punctuated with sometimes extensive periods of deceleration followed by years of very significant acceleration. What is interesting is that, but for two years in the late 1980s, China has recorded annual growth of more than 8 percent for over 30 years. Even the United States, generally labeled as one of the world's first emerging markets, did not enjoy such sustained economic expansion during its early years. Over the past 15 years, China alone has accounted for 40 percent of the increase in the world's industrial output. India, which is now second only to China in economic growth and investment opportunity, will need to expand by 8 percent annually for 15 years before it reaches a size comparable with that of China today.

China's stock indexes have produced stunning results since stock trading was introduced on the mainland (through the Shanghai and

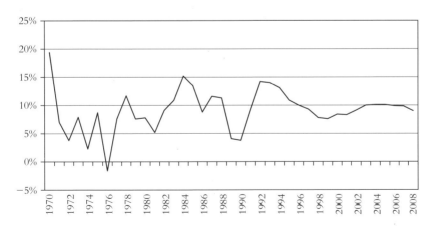

Figure 1.1 China's aggressive and remarkable 40-year GDP growth rate
SOURCE: Bloomberg

Shenzen exchanges) in the early 1990s. For foreign investors, however, it is the China H-shares listed in Hong Kong (which are mainland companies with listings on either Shanghai or Shenzen as well) and the Red Chips (which are mainland companies incorporated in Hong Kong and traded only in Hong Kong) that are of interest. Here the returns from the Hang Seng China Enterprises Index (HSCEI), which represents both H-shares and Red Chips, have been spectacular too, as shown in Figure 1.2.

The average annual return on the HSCEI between 1996 and 2009 has been 9.8 percent, as compared to a 5.7 percent return for the S&P 500, an annual loss of 3.3 percent for Japan's TOPIX, and a 13.8 percent annual average gain for India's NIFTY Index.

India's equity returns have been among the best over different time periods from 1991 (the year that India's reforms process began in earnest), producing annual returns of nearly 14 percent, more than double that of the S&P. Even from 1993 onward, when the Hong Kong Exchange began to trade Chinese enterprises, the best total stock returns have come from Indian stocks, with an annual return of 13 percent over that 16-year period. While the risk perception of the markets in emerging Asia is certainly justified, the potential for returns remains undiminished for several good reasons, as we shall see later.

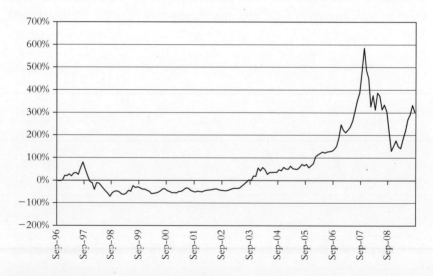

Figure 1.2   HSCEI returns, 1996–2009
SOURCE: Bloomberg

A New Economic Phase Begins for Asia

China's rise to prosperity in recent decades coincided with the surge in global trade and falling protectionism in major consuming regions. This trend led to extensive development of the coastal regions and cities that were the key to its economic strategy. But as the decade draws to a close, the economic structure that prevailed in the West for the previous five or six decades is beginning to look very different: the era of rapidly expanding global trade, open liberalism, and debt-funded consumerism is undergoing a drastic recalibration. Global economic relationships and national competitiveness are now being redefined in the wake of the global financial and trade crises that hit in 2007−08 as all nations seek to save more and protect their national economic interests by any means possible, giving rise to the specter of protectionism and reduced foreign trade.

Coincidentally, just as the developed economies face the prospect of years of slow growth and mediocre investment returns, East Asia— catalyzed by China—is entering the next phase of its modern economic era where the dominant themes will be linked to empowered domestic consumers and intra-regional trade. India for its part has long been focused on developing its domestic economy and has begun to accelerate that process. China has now begun to focus its collective energy on the development of its domestic market and its neglected hinterland. Given the lively pace of development and economic growth, Vietnam is being touted as the next Asian tiger and even Indonesia, East Asia's lumbering energy powerhouse always full of unrealized potential, is showing signs of breaking from the past and actually contributing to Asia's powerful growth story.

Significantly, the Chinese central government now sees the development of its domestic economy as a responsibility, not just to the Chinese people but to the rest of the world, and in keeping with its self-image as a "great and responsible" power. As China continues to open up its economy to competition through the slowdown it will become a powerful growth catalyst for a number of global economic sectors.

By Western standards the Asian consumer market has always been small, though growing rapidly for all that. Chinese growth has been driven by a high savings rate, a high investment rate, and low levels of domestic consumption. For China to supplant the US as a consumption-driven growth engine for the rest of the world then its historic trends must be reversed; consumption has to rise and savings fall. It seems as if a nation of frugal savers has now to turn into a nation of frantic shoppers. However, the unfortunate reality is that Chinese personal savings rates, especially in the more prosperous urban areas, had been falling long before the recent financial crises, and under the current economic circumstances, may not fall very much further. Chinese economists have been pointing out for some time now that individual Chinese savers are saving less than before and their place has gradually been taken by corporate and government consumption.

The Chinese government's understanding of this fact led to a swift and very aggressive direction to state-owned banks to step up lending to Chinese households at very low rates of interest. In addition, the Chinese government has implemented a corporate policy clearly designed to shore up domestic confidence (no pay cuts, no retrenchments, and no delays in payments to domestic suppliers) and one that quickly began to take effect in the second quarter of 2009, pushing domestic spending and raising global demand for metals, fuel, and other industrial commodities. India too unveiled a new economic policy, soon after national elections in May 2009 were convincingly won by incumbent reformist prime minister Dr. Manmohan Singh, that aggressively targets domestic growth, infrastructure spending, and increasing the government's financial flexibility. India is different from other Asian economies in that it has built an economy with a very strong domestic story and very low dependence on global trade and, despite the impact of contracting credit, it came into these crises very well positioned for growth.

Despite the forecast and expectation of strong growth rates for many Asian nations, how reasonable is the notion that these nations will move from being high savers to high spenders? Is there hope that the domestic markets in Asia and, especially, in China and India will provide the necessary growth momentum and a fillip to the global economy? And will Asian governments succeed with their plan to use their substantial financial flexibility (given that both households and most governments are underleveraged) and controlled banking systems to trigger a sharp but sustainable increase in credit and consumption?

These are questions that may appear hard to answer in the short term, but there are trends unfolding that make for some very powerful longer-term fundamental changes. Intra-Asian trade mechanisms are being strengthened in an unprecedented manner, with 35 bilateral and multilateral free-trade agreements (FTAs) negotiated between Asian countries in various stages of implementation. Second, almost every major nation in the world pulled out a stimulus package for their economies, together pumping between US$3–4 trillion into their recovery strategies. However, only India and China saw a powerful and quick resurgence in growth rates by the second quarter of 2009. While collectively the world economies—weighed down by the US, the Eurozone, and Japan—will experience a contraction for 2009 and small growth for 2010, only China and India among the major economies will push up toward their average growth rates. This is a powerful indicator of what the future might hold. It is almost certain that Japan's contribution to the Asian story will diminish over time. That role will be taken over by China, India, and the other large emerging economies of Indonesia and, possibly, Vietnam. Third, while the world has started wooing the Asian consumer, Asian companies are busy creating jobs across the world. Led once again by the indomitable Chinese, Asian companies are out there buying up corporate assets all over the place—from coal and iron-ore mines in Australia, auto-parts makers and auto plants in the US, equipment manufacturers and pharmaceutical plants in Europe, and oil projects in Canada, Africa, and Central America. According to an Ernst & Young study, between 2008 and 2009, some of the better-known Indian companies (including Reliance Communications, Wipro Technologies, and Tata Chemicals) made 143 acquisitions in the US alone, across a multitude of sectors including pharmaceuticals, IT, textiles, and manufacturing. One-third of these deals happened during the worst of the contraction in the US in 2009 and involved companies going bankrupt and about to close. In a similar vein, companies from other parts of Asia too have been buying up troubled companies in the US and elsewhere and essentially investing in those economies by saving jobs and keeping factories humming.

China's capital productivity has not compared well even with other fast-growing nations. China invests 40 percent of its GDP to produce a 9 percent growth rate; India on the other hand invests 30 percent of its GDP to produce an 8 percent growth rate. So unless there is an improvement in capital productivity, as the Chinese investment rate slows so will its GDP growth. In a sense there is a bit of a role reversal between India and China; where China drove its GDP growth through higher investments and lower consumption, India drove it through higher consumption and lower investments. Now India has been accelerating its investments just as China is accelerating its consumption. China has already built up very significant manufacturing capacities in a number of industries and will now have to spend locally to utilize that capacity. Indian companies have increasingly been driving investment spending in India and in general it would be reasonable to expect an upswing in corporate earnings growth following a period of sustained growth in capital expenditure.

Whether or not Asia actually delivers on the high expectations being placed on it, the world's reliance on the economic power of Asian nations to bring about a measure of stability is a remarkable turnaround from the situation a little over 10 years ago, when so much in rapidly growing Asian economies depended on the largesse of global multilateral financial institutions and the financial backing of the US and Japan. China's ability to influence the global economy is becoming more pronounced because of how it is using its wealth and knowledge in shaping a new pan-Asian economic framework focused on its domestic economy and inter-Asian trade. It is also triggering dramatic changes in North and Southeast Asia in particular and in the rest of the world in general. East Asian nations in particular are redefining their economic agenda and rapidly fine-tuning it to complement China's emerging domestic strategy.

Stock market returns from China, India, Japan, South Korea, Singapore, and Hong Kong have been superlative ever since Asian markets bottomed out in late October 2008 and have produced stunning absolute and relative returns (see Figure 1.3). As foreign investors became shaky participants during the global slowdown it was domestic investors that piled into mutual funds, especially in China where stocks have returned 25 percent. In India, the return has been 15 percent, as opposed to a -14 percent return in the US. It is very noteworthy that it

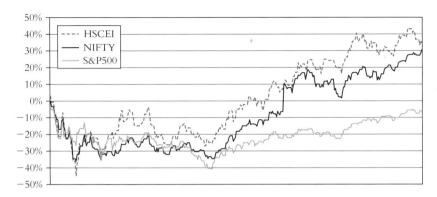

Figure 1.3 H-Shares (China), NIFTY Index (India) versus the S&P500
(October 08 – September 09)

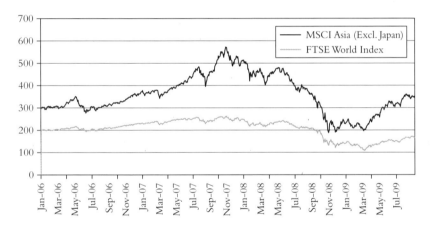

Figure 1.4 Emerging and developed-world markets compared

was the rally in China and key Asian markets that marked the bottom
for global stock indices in October 2008.

The US markets followed five months later, in March 2009. This
could signal the emergence of Asian markets as the trendsetters of
the global economy and stock markets. It is also not surprising that
declines or weakness in the leading Asian markets now tend to send
ripples across global markets.

As Figure 1.4 makes clear, even when other Asian markets (with
the exception of Japan) are included, the superior performance of

emerging Asia against that of the developed world equity markets before and after the 2008 crash is evident.

While questions and doubts may persist about Asia's past performance and its future potential, and while debate may rage about whether Asia (especially China) can replace the US consumer and thus save the whole world, this really misses the point. Real development has occurred in Asia with some very profound and fundamental changes, some evident and some not so. The real story in Asia therefore is the mega-trends and themes that have begun to unfold across the continent, some recent and some that have been decades in the making, that are the real source of opportunity and value for global investors. These themes and trends are set out in brief in the following sections and are discussed in greater detail later in the book.

Emerging Investment Themes in Asia

A Rapidly Rising Standard of Living and a Large and Growing Middle Class Well Positioned on the Road to Prosperity Is a Powerful Growth Trigger

Asia is now home to the fastest-growing economies anywhere, and key Asian nations have experienced rapid growth in GDP and per-capita income, sustained increases in asset prices, and a rising standard of living for the last two decades. Asian GDP has increased from US$8 trillion in 1995 to US$14 trillion in 2008 (an annual growth rate of 5.7 percent) and according to IMF estimates will reach US$20 trillion by 2014 (with an even faster annual growth rate of 7.1 percent). Consumerism is the new economic mantra for a population that is younger, better educated than ever before, with a growing disposable income and the confidence to use it. Their desire for an upwardly mobile existence is proving to be the ultimate growth trigger. By 2020 half of all Chinese will belong to the middle classes, while India and China together will add 450 million people to the ranks of the middle class by 2030. The greatest impact will be felt in the real-estate market, since it is every person's dream to own their own home (followed by owning their personal transportation).

Asian households (barring Japan and South Korea) in general are underleveraged and have discovered the purchasing power of the credit card. Given that India's and China's household debt/GDP ratio is barely over 10 percent, over the next few years we are likely to see the emergence of a new and aggressive breed of Asian consumer. This is likely to drive the values of companies that cater to the local economy and depend on domestic consumers of all types of goods and services. Sectors and companies that are dependent on discretionary spending, whether on consumer durables (including electronics, TVs, and automobiles), real estate, travel and leisure, media, and consumer staples such as food and beverage producers to general and specialty retailers, look to be promising. Equally strong and almost recession-proof is the education sector. Financial services and asset managers will be big beneficiaries as disintermediation takes hold and Asian countries relax regulations on intra-regional trade in financial services. Already brokerages in the region, and especially in China, have reported an unprecedented increase in new retail brokerage accounts during the trough and rally in 2009.

Multinational corporations with strong brands have already made sizeable inroads into key Asian markets; companies such as YUM! Brands, Coca-Cola, Procter & Gamble, Kellogg's, Nestlé, and Unilever, for example, have very successful platforms in Asia, from which they will derive a growing portion of their future revenues. GM, a company synonymous with a sick manufacturing sector in the US, is the number-one foreign car maker in China, with a 13 percent market share in what is surely the world's most fragmented passenger-car market. GM reported nearly 40 percent volume growth in China during the first half of 2009, even as it emerged from bankruptcy in the US. GM expects to double its current volume in China alone to two million by 2014.

A key measure to look for will be per-capita income growth, and the disposable share of that income is expected to increase exponentially. In the last couple of decades China has increased its per-capita income several fold. If India invests heavily in infrastructure and carries out necessary structural reforms, it can easily be a US$55 trillion economy by 2050 and raise annual per-capita income from the US$1,200 reported in 2008 to US$36,500. Countries such as Vietnam too have

Table 1.1 Per-capita income growth for select Asian economies

Country	1987–1997	1997–2007	2006	2007	2007–2011
China	8.9%	8.7%	11.0%	11.2%	9.7%
India	5.5%	6.9%	8.2%	7.7%	7.2%
Indonesia	6.1%	2.3%	4.3%	5.1%	5.2%
Malaysia	6.5%	2.5%	4.0%	4.0%	4.3%
Vietnam	5.6%	5.9%	6.9%	7.2%	6.9%

SOURCE: World Bank

done an excellent job at pulling up living standards and are likely to accelerate that trend. The growth in per-capita incomes (actual and projected) for selected Asian economies is set out in Table 1.1.

Education is a booming business in China, India, Korea, and other parts of emerging Asia. For a continent with a young population, education is both a government priority and a multi-billion-dollar opportunity being quickly exploited by entrepreneurial and well-established companies alike, including the likes of Disney, Pearson Plc, and Linguaphone.

India has neglected its basic education system but has spent heavily on higher technical education, producing world-class institutes such as the six Indian Institutes of Technology (IITs) and thus preparing itself well for a service-oriented economy. India's development of the Tejas multi-role fighter aircraft showcased the depth of its scientific and engineering talent. Led by the public-sector aviation company Hindustan Aeronautics Ltd., more than 100 national research laboratories (including the Gas Turbine Research Establishment, National Aerospace Laboratories, private companies' research divisions, and engineering institutes) worked on cutting-edge technologies ranging from developing composite materials for the air frame, multi-mode radar, and a highly versatile jet engine. The Aeronautical Development Agency, which has oversight over the project, has licensed out some of the key technologies developed to global aircraft manufacturers and software companies.

China, on the other hand, prepared itself well for an industrial economy by focusing very zealously on primary education for all.

Though the emphasis on higher technical education is a newer phenomenon, China is not without its science-and-technology laboratories and its world-class companies that can now drive its industrial might. China too has a very long history of scientific innovation and technological progress. The Ming Dynasty voyages mentioned earlier are just one example of its demonstrated pursuit of technical prowess. The largest ships in those fleets, measuring roughly 500 feet in length and housing a thousand people, were considered to be the largest and most sophisticated sea-faring vessels of the time.

In comparing the development of the two nations, it may be easy to overlook the fact that in several ways India resembles a post-industrial society, with its advanced knowledge-based industries and remarkable technical prowess even in nascent areas such as nanotechnology and advanced aerospace technology. China has furiously pursued advanced scientific development and after two decades of effort has only just caught up with India in its annual output of scientific manpower.

Asia Is Urbanizing at an Unprecedented Pace

Asia is turning itself into an urbanized society, and several nations have begun to display the characteristics of post-industrial economies. This transformation is not simply a shift from a predominantly agrarian economic model to a predominantly industrial one but a shift of the labor force away from agriculture and into industrial and, more importantly, service sectors, thus significantly boosting overall wages and the standard of living.

Of all the major economies, India still has the largest proportion of its population in rural areas. China offers a good, large-scale model for India to follow in shifting its manpower away from agriculture into better-paying industrial jobs and from rural to urban areas. Despite the superior quality of its services sector, around 57 percent of the total Indian workforce is still engaged in agricultural and rural-based activities even though 75 percent of GDP is generated by the industrial and services sectors. India is now back-pedaling and creating the necessary economic environment to strengthen its industrial base like East Asia has done. The model that India has developed is built around the quality of its manpower and the high levels of technology absorption that will enable it to grow quickly into a post-industrial society. True prosperity will come when India is able to meaningfully employ its rural population and scale up its industrial base.

The 1990s was a period of change for most of Asia and its economic and social direction that has been driving rapid industrialization and the building of a strong and well-organized service economy. In 1991 India shed its socialist past and began reforms in earnest, while China's accelerated growth led to its accession to the WTO and the opening of its domestic economy. Following the Asian financial crisis of 1997–98 East Asia put in place numerous changes that transformed its economies; and a decade of weak oil prices prompted very significant change in thinking in the Middle East, where the move away from oil has begun in earnest, prompting the development of an urbanized service economy encompassing tourism and financial services.

To that end, growing urbanization in almost all Asian economies is a driver of economic growth, especially given all the ancillary trends that it triggers. The shift from rural to urban living results in more development initiatives that go beyond real estate and infrastructure and drive a number of other sectors. Social shift involves changes in how people choose to live, a reduction in average family size, a rise in incomes, and an increase in disposable surplus to spend on discretionary goods.

Growing Regional Cooperation and Economic Integration—A Mass Market Opens to Local Trade

The East Asian nations (Japan, South Korea, Taiwan, Singapore, and Thailand) that rose to prominence on their substantive trading volumes with the United States, now count China as their single biggest and most influential trading partner. Japan's foreign-trade statistics are the most telling symbol of this change. Up until 2008, the United States had always been Japan's largest trading partner, but then China claimed that title. China's total trade with Japan amounts to nearly US$260 billion per annum while Japan's total trade with the US is US$240 billion. Even China's trade with India has grown by 32 percent annually for the last 10 years. These trends become more significant when we consider that after being stung hard by the economic slump, US consumers have cut back on consumption rather drastically. A portion of this lost spending will be felt in global trade, with the biggest loser being China, which will need its trading partners in Asia like never before to help keep its factories humming. It will also be forced to open up its own economy to further competition. This unprecedented economic need is probably the best guarantee that China will do its utmost to promote economic stability in Asia and will seek further integration and cooperation among Asian economies, a process that has been under way for several years now. Essentially this process will provide preferred and less-cumbersome access for Asian companies to rapidly expanding Asian economies.

Asian regional cooperation and economic integration, which has become critical to global recovery, has been on the rise for several years and is now at an unprecedented level. It will rise to even greater heights in the years ahead. In 1980, a little over one-third of Asian trade was within Asia; at present this figure is approaching 60 percent. The activation of the ASEAN–China free trade area (FTA) in 2010 will create the world's largest trading bloc and will supersede the European Union in impact (if not in scale since the EU GDP is around US$18 trillion). It will encompass 1.7 billion people directly and nearly 3 billion people through linked agreements such as the ASEAN–India FTA, the China–India FTA, the India–Korea FTA, and the China–Korea–Japan economic framework and trade agreements—which will cover half the world's population, nearly a third of world GDP (at nearly US$13 trillion), and all the world's fastest-growing economies. The ASEAN–China FTA alone will have an annual GDP of nearly US$5 trillion and well over a trillion dollars of intra-regional trade. India too has put into effect its "look East" policy through which it intends to foster very close links with East Asia. All of these changes to how the most powerful Asian nations now interact and trade with each other will, through sheer dynamism and accelerating growth, shift the levers of economic power to the Asia-Pacific region. However, given other competing national priorities, a single standardized economic union along the lines of the EU may be much further off since it is a little difficult to envisage Asian collaboration on important issues such as defense and foreign policy.

While the ASEAN nations (10 Southeast Asian nations), South Korea, Greater China (China, Taiwan, Singapore, and Hong Kong), Japan, and India are looking at lifting all barriers to intra-regional trade, it is the movement of people between these nations for leisure rather than work that will likely be an enduring investment theme for a long time to come. The Japanese and South Koreans have long been the region's most avid travelers, especially to each other's countries and to the West. But now a new force has emerged on the Asian tourist scene; the Chinese traveler. Chinese global tourism is only a recent phenomenon and for a while people could travel freely only to those countries that had been approved by the Chinese government. But this is no longer an issue, and most nations have now been approved and the rush to East Asia is well under way.

On the western fringe of Asia lie the desert kingdoms of the Gulf Cooperation Council (GCC) nations (Saudi Arabia, Kuwait, United Arab Emirates, Qatar, Oman, and Bahrain). These nations have functioned as a trading bloc since 1981 and are now pursuing the creation of a common currency, already a much-delayed event but likely to take effect within the next five years following the launch of their common market in January 2008. These are all probable precursors to eventual economic union. These six nations are also looking toward a future when their economic reliance on oil revenues will reduce, and today are looking to develop the region into a services and hospitality hub, with tourism as a cornerstone of their new investment strategy. These two broad economic trends unfolding in East and West Asia are likely to see the emergence of two very dynamic economic and consumer blocs in Asia that will drive growth and create interesting investment opportunities across a wide swathe of the continent.

It has almost become economic dogma in the Western investment world to believe in the BRIC (Brazil, Russia, India, and China) economic mantra and that China will be the world's largest economy by 2050 and India the second-largest. The probability of that actually happening is not very relevant in gauging where the investment opportunity lies in these economies and which investment is likely to endure over the long term. The fact of the matter is that these two countries currently define and envelop a lot of the economic and investment transformation in Asia and the world since the 1990s. But while these two giant economies contribute to Asian growth and political stability, they also benefit from the tremendous strides taken by several other Asian economies since the economic shock of the debt and currency crisis in 1997–98. A development not recognized in the BRIC argument, but one that is a distinct reality today, is the heightened economic integration and cooperation between various blocs of Asian nations. This process of integration builds on the region's competitive advantages, thus making the entire region, and not just one or two countries within it, a very compelling investment story. As economic integration becomes more robust and financial integration becomes an important element, the depth, sophistication, and opportunities within these economies will also grow.

Evolution of a Robust Pan-Asian Financial Infrastructure

Without discounting the seriousness of the economic pain felt in Asia as a result of the global financial crisis in 2008–09, the defining crisis for many emerging Asian nations was the 1997 currency and debt crisis. That crisis quickly turned into a severe economic contraction for several Southeast and North Asian nations. East Asian nations suffered dramatic economic collapse, including a run on their currencies. Aided and supported largely by Japan, the US, and an emerging China, the crisis drove the resurgence of a new Asian economic system based less on state direction and more on free-market economics and competition. The focus was on economic management and on building a more robust economic model capable of withstanding economic shocks. As a result, several of these countries emerged stronger, with more versatile and flexible domestic economies. Accumulating foreign-currency reserves has been the unrelenting focus of Asian governments, and their economic policies have evolved to sustain that objective. Asian nations today control the largest accumulation of dollar reserves anywhere in the world, with the bulk (a cumulative total of US$5–6 trillion) being concentrated in China, Japan, India, Singapore, and the GCC nations, and have the best-capitalized banks anywhere.

One very significant reason why Asia has escaped the worst of the 2008 financial crisis is that, with the exception of Japan and to some

degree South Korea, the financial sector, which is deeply embedded
in the fabric of more-developed societies, has not yet become a significant part of the economy, and the impact of economic contraction
is thus not carried as far. India is one of the best-placed countries in
respect of household debt and corporate leverage. Indian households
have one of the lowest mortgage penetration rates among any major
global economy—roughly 4–5 percent of GDP, where the average for
major Asian economies including Japan is around 28 percent. China's
is a little less than half of that. Indian companies too de-leveraged early
on, and, with the resulting reduction in the risk premium demanded,
Indian companies have considerably strengthened their balance sheets
with equity capital. Low leverage is one of the most significant reasons
why growth in Asia has already restarted (Japan being a notable exception) and why the more developed world will find it hard to keep pace
(as reducing its considerable debt will take a very long time).

Further, contrast the cohesive response from governments in Asia
to the economic and financial crisis with that in emerging Europe and
Latin America. Government or, for that matter, any institutional inter-
vention has largely been bilateral or through the Asian Development
Bank or other regional structures. There has been no recourse to the
International Monetary Fund (IMF) and, for the first time, Asian
nations other than Japan have actually been contributing to the IMF
capital base. This means that Asian governments today have the financial flexibility needed to spur growth with a further dose of stimulus
spending if needed. China in particular enjoys a high proportion of tax
receipts to GDP and low fiscal deficits as well as public debt.

Along with these changes, also emerging is a shift in financial centers. London rose to become the world's financial capital in the eighteenth and nineteenth centuries, replacing Amsterdam and Lisbon.
New York was propelled into the same role in the twentieth century
and remains the leader today. But, increasingly, Shanghai is being positioned as one the world's great emerging financial centers, along with
Seoul, Singapore, and Abu Dhabi. Shanghai is already at the center of
Asia's very significant and growing corporate-bond market, valued at
some US$43 trillion.

An even more important and symbiotic development is the push
to reduce barriers to intra-Asian trade in financial services. There is

a growing awareness of this need for further Asian integration among Asian central bankers and financial institutions. Though still in its early stages, this could be one very exciting trend which, as it unfolds, adds further depth to the Asian financial system in general and capital markets in particular. India and China are today considered to be the world's foremost emerging markets for financial services. The prospects for the insurance sector are very strong, with most nations reporting very low levels of insurance penetration but strong potential given a better appreciation of risk and the growing sophistication of products offered, especially in retirement and healthcare segments.

Today with the Western world's financial system and once-vaunted banks in shambles, the most valuable banks by market capitalization are now Chinese banks. At the time of writing, the International Commercial Bank of China (ICBC) is the world's most valuable bank, with a market capitalization of US$175 billion. Before the start of the crisis in late 2007, Citigroup alone was worth US$250 billion, before losing 95 percent of its value. It therefore came as no surprise when the governor of the Chinese central bank made an uncharacteristically bold statement that China was better poised to lead the global recovery since its financial system and institutions were stronger than most.

Development of a Strong and Growing Private Sector

Unlike most other Asian nations, with the possible exception of Indonesia, India has single-mindedly focused on developing its domestic economy for decades. While India and China had similar backgrounds and economic and political conditions in the 1950s when they began their respective socialist and communist journeys, their paths began to diverge almost immediately. India stayed true to its commitment to build a hybrid economic model of private and state enterprise, where the state undertook the arduous task of building heavy industry, education, and infrastructure and the private sector did everything else. However, the Indian government began to make its overbearing presence felt on the private sector's turf by the 1970s, when the nationalization of banks and other industries reached a higher pitch, culminating with the forced departure of foreign companies such as Coca-Cola and others. Those companies that did not leave had to dilute equity in favor of domestic retail investors and list on Indian exchanges. Even during the darkest days of state control, the Indian private sector continued to grow even as companies sought government patronage and entrenched players succeeded in keeping out competition. This phenomenon allowed the blossoming of several private conglomerates and turned them into industrial behemoths. Indian managers, companies, and brands continued to develop and, more importantly, the institutional infrastructure also developed, thus aiding the development of the private sector. So when India's experiment with socialism and nationalization ended in 1991 and the economy was re-opened to foreign competition in 1993, the stage was set for a tremendous release of entrepreneurial energy and a ramping up of the institutional infrastructure.

In contrast, China grew only state-owned corporations and thus lacked a history of strong private-sector growth. Everything remained in the hands of the government until recently and even now the bulk of industry is state controlled or state driven. China remained mired in the communist dogma of central planning and state ownership and control of all economic levers until the late 1970s, and for a long time even after liberalization the state maintained control of nearly the entire economy. However, from the mid-1990s there began to emerge a growing entrepreneurial layer within the domestic economy that is beginning to transform the state-dominated economic model into a hybrid economy, more like India's. Recent surveys of the Chinese job market have shown that one in four Chinese intend to be self-employed. As recently as 2003 China did not have a single billionaire on the Forbes list; by 2009 it had 28, edging India (with 24) into second place on the Asian billionaires list.

The reason why until recently India had had a larger number of billionaires despite China's economy being three times larger is that India's private sector represents a much larger percentage of its economy. Indian private industry has been around since the early 1900s, and well before independence from Britain in 1947 the Indian private sector controlled steel and cement plants, airlines, hotels, insurance companies, and banks. By 2009, the Indian private sector was contributing more than US$800 billion to GDP as compared to the US$600 billion contribution from the Chinese private sector, despite being one-third the size of China's GDP. The Indian planning commission has said that for India's 11th Five Year Plan (2007–12), the private sector's investment share will be 80 percent. The Indian market capitalization also is largely dominated by privately run firms (67 percent of a US$1 trillion market cap) and currently has some 7,000 listed companies, as compared to 1,500 listings on Shenzen and Shanghai combined (though when Chinese companies in Hong Kong, Singapore, Toronto, and the American Depository Reciepts [ADRs] in NYSE and NASDAQ are taken into account this will be a larger number).

In addition, Indian public-equities markets provide investors with the option of buying into local listings of global corporations. For example, GlaxoSmithKline, Siemens, ABB, Unilever, Proctor & Gamble, Nestlé, Ingersoll Rand, Bosch, ITW, and a large number of other global corporations have listed their subsidiaries in India and offer a serious alternative to global investors looking for high-quality exposure to India. China still has to go beyond the heft of government companies and needs to make its markets more conducive to foreign companies listing subsidiary companies in China.

While India has had a head start in building world-class companies, the Chinese have learned very quickly and now have some dynamic companies with few ties to the state that are able to hold their own in a domestic economy that is increasingly competitive. Taiwan is a good example of the interplay between the state and the businesses it spawns. While promoting industries such as semiconductors over the past three decades, the Taiwanese also created an environment for a thriving private sector and built strong institutional frameworks to enable interplay between the government, the private sector, and Taiwan's strong technical universities. The government also fostered the spirit of competition and cooperation with the Taiwanese private sector. As a result of its very forward-looking economic policies and early development of its human capital (which, incidentally, was a function of Japanese government policy during its occupation of Taiwan during the Second World War), Taiwan has reported one of the most phenomenal per-capita GDP growth rates (12 percent annually from 1962 to 2008), with per-capita GDP (adjusted for purchasing power parity) increasing from US$170 to US$33,000. Its level of development and economic growth has put Taiwan on par with developed nations.

Privatization, the New Growth Engine

For any economy to prosper, it has to be driven by private enterprise and by entrepreneurs seeking a profit, surviving competition, and innovating. Russia is a good example of a state that has not been able to let go of its control over the economy and one that keeps muddying the playing field for private enterprise. By contrast, the relatively recent hybrid Chinese model of state-directed capitalism has proven to be a good incubator of entrepreneurship. Most Chinese enterprises begin with state support, including ample, low-cost credit, and are allowed to grow before being turned over to private hands. Carefully nurtured entrepreneurship in combination with financial stability, labor flexibility, and consistent economic and monetary policies have become the foundations of a successful economic system. Added to this, there has been a recognition of the need for independent regulatory bodies. The successful creation of such bodies in the securities industry (for example, the China Securities Regulatory Commission, the China Banking Regulatory Commission, and the China Insurance Regulatory Commission) makes the case for investors all the more compelling.

The extent of private ownership of the Chinese economy will increase as state-owned enterprises privatize and new enterprises are spawned or IPOs are launched by the private sector. In India, too, privatization is expected to pick up. Expectations among global investors are running high in the aftermath of the 2009 national elections that the Indian government will aggressively privatize state-owned companies. The fact that several such companies have come forward with plans to raise equity from domestic and overseas capital markets provides a basis for investor optimism. In the five-year period before the 2009 elections, the Indian government was hampered by its leftist coalition partners who blocked any talk of privatization and was thus not able to build on the significant momentum given to privatization by the previous government led by Atal Behari Vajpayee (1999–2004). (Even highly developed Asian economies such as Taiwan still have a very significant proportion of state-owned enterprises, though the Taiwanese government has said very clearly that it intends to privatize most of these.)

In India's case, the companies that are most in need of growth capital are the state-owned banks, oil companies, and power companies, which should be among the enterprises most likely to reduce the government's stake as they raise capital. There are 48 government-owned companies listed on the Indian exchanges, with a current market value exceeding US$400 billion. Speculation that the new Indian government will move quickly to privatize or further reduce its stake in listed non-bank companies has driven returns from the beginning of 2009, though it is likely that some outperforming banks (such as Corporation Bank) will be candidates for disinvestment.

The decision by various Middle East governments to privatize state-owned assets and allow foreign investors to participate has already created a sizeable securities market for their assets, both in GDP and absolute terms. The GCC nations now command a market capitalization of nearly US$600 billion, over 50 percent of which is Saudi Arabian and nearly one-quarter Kuwaiti. However, the investible universe for foreign investors is small in these markets and there are a number of restrictions, especially in Saudi Arabia, which has little foreign-investor participation. The most investor-friendly markets are the UAE, Kuwait, and Qatar, which between them have more than half the region's investible total. The privatization trend is expected to continue in the Gulf Arab nations and will form the basis for long-term institutional-investor interest and eventual participation in their economies.

Increased privatization and increased private-sector activity that, in turn, engenders competition will be among the great drivers for much of the region, especially China and India. China's acknowledgment of the need for competition, especially foreign competition on the mainland, began to accelerate after it joined the WTO in 2001. According to Chinese government statistics, nearly 15,000 new entities, both domestic and foreign, are registered every year. As more foreign companies set up operations in China, not just to export overseas but to service and sell to the domestic economy, the relative importance of China to the rest of the world will only increase. Besides offering the world a greater stake in its growth story, more economic openness is a terrific tool with which to build strong and resilient domestic companies, as India's experience has shown. If India today is able to boast companies that can compete with the best in the world in diverse industries such as steel, automobiles, pharmaceuticals, chemicals, telecommunications, and IT, this is largely due to the brutal competition that these and other sectors were subjected to both from imports (lower tariff barriers) and from foreign companies that invested in India from the early 1990s as a result of the government's economic liberalization program. And this has been the case across Asia, where foreign direct investment (FDI) and less-restrictive import regimes have become enablers of economic prosperity.

Infrastructure Development and Energy Security as Mega-Economic Drivers

Asia's hunger for energy is common knowledge. Decades of rapid development regardless of the impact on the environment is evident across the continent but especially in China. Asia is faced with the unpalatable task of maintaining the pace of its development while acknowledging that it has to contribute to mitigating the effects of global warming. There is no easy answer but both the scale of its energy requirements and the problem it faces have become a huge investment catalyst for both conventional and renewable energy.

Asian nations led by China and India have already commenced plans to invest well over a trillion dollars into power, roads, ports, airports, telecom, water, sanitation, and other physical infrastructure projects to be put into place across the continent over the next few years. The focus of these projects will be determined by their respective national priorities. China's focus is on water management and supply, power, and expanding its railway network; Indonesia's is on transportation infrastructure; in the GCC countries it's tourist infrastructure; while in India it is still core infrastructure of roads, ports, railways, and power. Given the large number of projects already announced or in the planning stages, Asia is emerging as one of the biggest customers of the global renewable energy and nuclear industries.

Vast sums are being poured into energy infrastructure whether it be gas pipelines in the central Asian republics, liquefied natural gas terminals, or cryogenic carriers to refineries (the largest of which is now in Asia). Currently there are 37 re-gasification terminals in Asia (28 of which are in Japan, three in India, and one in China), with 40 more being built in the Asia-Pacific region with Japan, India, and China dominating the demand. China, India, Korea, and Japan are major emerging markets for nuclear power and there are a number of global companies in the engineering, construction, mining, and fuel-supply businesses that will benefit from Asia's unprecedented plans to invest in nuclear energy.

Asian Economies and Corporations Are an Integral Part of Global Industrial and Services Networks

Given the powerful development trends seen within Asian economies, most Asian companies are less likely to be hurt by global disruptions and more likely to contribute to the recovery. For most global corporations too, China and India have become pivotal to their growth strategies, and establishing business relationships and lucrative supply contracts is now essential. Today it is unthinkable for the global IT industry to contemplate growing its business without being integrated with India's software companies or its vast software talent pool. Similarly, for hardware manufacturers integration with the Taiwanese semiconductor industry is critical. Taiwan's evolution as a hardware manufacturer began in the 1980s, when it acted as an outsourcer for American and Japanese technology companies. Taiwanese companies, backed by the government, focused on semiconductor technologies. Companies such as UMC and Taiwan Semiconductor Manufacturing Company, which began with technology transfer to set up chip foundries, have now grown into technology leaders and created entire industry and sub-industry clusters including chip-design houses, a whole slew of semiconductor device manufacturers, and device assemblers. Intense competition within the Taiwanese semiconductor and hardware clusters and very strong linkages between companies and technical universities have resulted in an entire innovation-support infrastructure that includes funding for start-ups. Today, Taiwanese companies are leading the global drive in optoelectronics. Touch-screen technologies, the kind that made the iPhone all the rage, owe their success in part to the development efforts and innovation of several Taiwanese companies.

This is true for a host of other industries that have integrated actively with Asian companies and sectors—including consumer goods, electronics, auto assembly, heavy industrial equipment, chemicals, and pharmaceuticals, to name but a few.

Being a critical part of the supply chain is one part of the story; the other is being integral to the future growth path of global companies. For example, Linde, a large European industrial-gases company, revealed that almost all its growth now comes from emerging Europe and Asia, and the scale of its involvement with Asia—especially India, China, and emerging industrial centers such as Abu Dhabi—is now unprecedented, with long-term contracts from core industries in metals, oil, and gas running into the billions of dollars. For industries ranging from footwear manufacturing to high-end electronics and from pharmaceuticals to integrated circuits, Asian companies are at the center of it all.

Reaping the Benefits of Political Stability, Improving Regulatory Infrastructure, and Corporate-Governance Practices

To complement their growing incomes and favorable demographics, most Asian societies (including China) now have greater social, economic, and political freedoms than ever before to enjoy their new-found wealth. Democracy today is certainly far more widespread in Asia than ever before, even though autocratic and single-party rule still remains even within nominally democratic frameworks. Despite the presence of all types of regimes, Asia is more politically stable and peaceful than it has been for many years. At the same time, we are witnessing a rapid development of institutional frameworks in politics, trade, finance, and investments, which are essential elements for regional stability.

The change in regulatory environment has been felt most in China, especially in civil jurisprudence, where until recently there was a complete absence of legal infrastructure that was acceptable by any global standard. Contrary to popular opinion outside of China, Chinese citizens have more social and economic freedoms today that ever before; it is hard to forget that China before communism was a feudal society that parlayed the labor of many into riches for a few. In 1970, 64 percent of the Chinese population lived below the poverty line (defined by the World Bank as an income of less than a dollar a day). Today that figure is less than 10 percent of the population.

Even though income inequality remains very high, China has done a remarkable job in providing for its people.

The Chinese are empowered to bring lawsuits against their government and have been doing so with varying degrees of success for almost two decades. The degree of social and economic freedoms in China is of great importance simply because of its growing presence in the world and how it engages not only with developed nations such as the US but also with regional rivals such as India and Japan.

Though India and Israel are at the other end of the political spectrum (with multi-party democracies that have strong grassroots traditions), they are proof that fractious politics and sometimes dysfunctional coalition governments need not be impediments to development and growth. Indonesia, the Philippines, Taiwan, and even the once war-torn Cambodia have seen a string of stabilizing national elections and have already begun to earn dividends from that stability.

Corporate-governance practices have taken giant strides, which should greatly influence the way Asian stocks are valued in the future. Historically, equity risk premiums demanded of Asian markets were significantly high. Now the factors that drove those premiums are being addressed. Liquidity is improving as companies raise capital and dilute the shareholdings of founding families. The number of individual companies listed and traded will continue to increase as privatization gathers momentum and markets become accessible to a larger number of companies. There is a growing awareness of corporate-governance practices, and a better understanding of investor expectations and the link to value creation, all of which will eventually lead to a reduced risk premium demanded from the larger Asian economies.

Asia Rising: The Complete Picture

While the Asian giants, China, Korea, Japan, and India, are focused on their domestic economies and the race for growth is on in earnest, there are fundamental changes happening in other regions and nations on the continent that need to be understood. Despite the Middle East producing 40 percent of the world's oil and sitting on a large portion of the world's known oil and gas reserves, that region is often thought of as an investment backwater. Now its leading cities like Dubai (despite severe financial problems), Abu Dhabi, Manama, and Doha are positioning themselves as international financial, trade, and tourist centers, and are attracting not only investments in real estate but also establishing more demanding and transparent corporate-governance, legal, and financial systems.

The stunning rise and fall of the leveraged real-estate market there does not help dispel the perception of an immature and untested economic system. But the collapse of the real-estate market in "glitter cities" such as Dubai will only strengthen the determination of governments to de-couple their economic fortunes from oil. For example, the real-estate boom in Dubai took off largely as a result of a relaxation in the investment policies that were designed to promote the development of the financial sector as well as promote tourism as the new investment mantra. Those efforts are likely to outlast the real-estate bubble and the current contraction in tourist traffic in those regions. The emirate of Abu Dhabi is undergoing the greatest transformation. Backed by vast oil wealth and the world's largest pool of investment funds this city is being positioned as the world's premier cultural and financial center.

Reverberations from the global economic crisis are also forcing once-insular capital-exporting nations such as Kuwait to become picky about where they put their money. Bowing to political pressure at home, Kuwait has stopped investing overseas altogether and is focusing on national priorities. It has, for example, recently backed out of commitments to purchase the polymers business from Dow and to increase its stake in German car maker Daimler. This thinking could become more mainstream among the GCC capital exporters as the opportunities within their own borders exceed opportunities elsewhere.

While there is no real depth to the equity markets in the Middle East, there is a growing choice of investment names available for consideration by investors. These are largely concentrated in industries such as petrochemicals (with a huge competitive advantage in feedstock), banking and insurance, fertilizers (where a significant competitive advantage is the cost of feedstock), and telecommunications. Even though the restrictions on foreign investors are more than a little onerous right now, the Middle East could throw up some interesting investment opportunities a few years down the line.

That the Middle East countries can embark on these ambitious new economic plans and invest heavily within their borders is the result of the unprecedented political stability that many of them now enjoy. With the exception of Saudi Arabia, which is racked by domestic violence and a huge wealth gap, the Arabian Peninsula as a whole enjoys greater political cohesion and loyalty to their respective monarchs.

The Sun Rises in East Asia

The economic development in China over the past three decades is something of a double-edged sword for much of East Asia. On the one hand, China's ascendancy and the shift of manufacturing to the Chinese mainland has begun the process of hollowing out Southeast Asian manufacturing, especially of the lower value-added kind that depends more on labor cost and productivity. At the same time, though, it has also offered new opportunities for those nations to sell to China, especially intermediate- and higher-value-added manufactured goods, services, and technology.

The growing Chinese influence over Asia's trade flows did not happen by chance. Japan was the first Asian nation to reach developed status by using lower labor costs and manufacturing efficiencies, since the 1960s to focus on exports. Manufacturing momentum then flowed to the four Asian Tigers—Singapore, Hong Kong, Taiwan, and South Korea—which followed the Japanese example and created solid trade links with the US and Europe largely in consumer electronics and other manufactured goods such as textiles, footwear, integrated circuits, and semiconductors. China in turn learned very quickly that exports was the way to go and built its model, buoyed less by productivity and more by its greater labor-cost advantage, on the products and strengths already created by Japan and the Asian Tigers and by the shift of manufacturing from Southeast Asia to the Chinese mainland. However, the breadth of products that China makes now far exceeds anything produced by the other East Asian economies, though electronics exports account for a little over one-fifth of Chinese total exports. This was both a threat and an opportunity for Japan and the Tiger economies: they quickly saw China's advantages and began to focus on China as the preferred destination for their exports, and imports of intermediate goods from China for their own manufacturing industry. Nearly half of Taiwanese exports to China, for example, comprise electromechanical or optoelectronic products.

Malaysia has demonstrated that such a shift away from a raw-material export-based economy to a modern industrial and service economy is well within the realm of possibility. The strategies that Malaysia used to effect this (improve education, infrastructure, political stability, and state sponsorship of industries) are being emulated by others. In the 20 years that have elapsed since Malaysia moved away from being a raw-material supplier to the world it has developed competitiveness in several industries and in not all of these does it possess a natural competitive advantage. The Malaysian economy is now readying itself for the next phase of development where it is looking to build its information technology and pharmaceutical sectors.

Cambodia is another example of emerging investment potential if the government and politicians can turn the hard-won peace and nearly two decades of a functioning democratic process into real economic gains. It has a fairly well-developed textile segment, dominated by overseas companies taking advantage of the country's cheap labor and abundant supply of raw materials, but also has tremendous potential in mining for both iron ore and precious stones. However, it remains daunting for individual investors to take advantage of the opportunity in Cambodia since there is no market for securities (unlike in the Middle East where, though opportunities will unfold over the next decade as they build up their internal governance systems, they still do have an existing public market for securities for those investors who wish to venture there).

Though there remains a long way to go, several significant lessons have been learned from past crises and much has already been achieved. High savings rates, strong GDP growth, the emphasis on domestic consumption, high investment rates, and capital formation are all the envy of the world. No wonder then that most people in Asia resent the fact that they too suffered the effects of financial troubles conceived elsewhere but that washed up on their shores nonetheless. Countries which, like Indonesia, are heavily dependent on the resource sector will probably be hard hit if commodity prices do not pick up. A recent survey of FDI flows throughout the world shows that nations with a large resource or financial exposure will suffer the worst in the case of a prolonged downturn. But, as we will see later, the crisis that unfolded globally is not a terrible tragedy for the continent and especially its stronger nations.

The objective of this book is to examine opportunities in Asia. Given the role that China is playing and its recent evolution and historical position, we will logically focus significantly on the opportunity there. But I will add one caveat to an unfolding Asian age of prosperity led by China. China has in the past rejected both its own prosperity and its leadership role in world political or economic spheres. Its history has shown that China alone can restrict China's ascendancy. While it is the likely super-heavyweight champion in our lifetime, India, too, is rising to a position of eminence, and Japan will retain its own sphere of influence. Add to this mix the growing dynamism in economies such as Indonesia, Vietnam, Malaysia, and the Philippines; re-calibrated growth in Israel; and unprecedented economic diversity emerging in a few of the Middle Eastern economies and we have the making of a truly Asian century, as opposed to the notion of a Chinese or Indo-Chinese century that has become commonplace in popular investment thinking.

Asian society has not progressed evenly since several nations began taking tentative steps to develop in the early 1980s. The disparity in approaches and growth among different Asian countries and the distribution and pace of prosperity within nations remain uneven at best. Asian poverty remains very significant despite huge gains made by China and India. So, by focusing all its energy on developing its domestic market and aiming for more equitable distribution of income and wealth, China is once again leading Asia by example. And the domestic-wealth effect too is not widespread even within those nations where reform has been heeded. Needless to say there are huge shortcomings in each of these economies and regions. It is precisely these shortcomings and the amount of developmental work that remains to be done that will provide investors in Asia and the rest of the world with great investment opportunities.

Despite the sense of optimism regarding the opportunities that Asia presents, there are risks to be considered too. Despite the fact that many Asian economies have managed themselves well in recent years, there remain considerable risks—political, regulatory, and operating—that have the potential to derail some of the expected returns from this market. Many of Asia's recent top performers such as India and Vietnam suffer from growing pains where the physical infrastructure is simply not able to keep pace with the changes taking place. China is facing a desperate water and environmental crisis that some observers believe could lead to political crises. Southeast Asia is seeing an increase in risk in its manufacturing industries, while Vietnam, in a rare departure from recent Asian stability, is facing a serious shortage of foreign exchange.

Where India still lags behind most of East and Southeast Asia, despite creating a successful and unique model of its own, is in creating a more business-friendly environment. Even in outsourcing, its core competency, it still takes innumerable permits from all levels of government to begin operations in an urban center. In trying to create a workers' utopia in its flawed experiment with socialism, it has made it expensive, if not outright impossible, for companies to fire workers in a cost-effective manner. In China, supposedly the world's bastion of communist ideology, it is a relatively trivial matter to let employees go or restructure enterprises. Despite India's inevitable and very significant rise, it may not be in a position to challenge China in too many spheres at the moment. This book examines the dynamics that drive the differences in these two countries: democratic but dysfunctional India; autocratic but very capable China.

For a rising power like India the continuing rise of China will be a wake-up call. While India can rise in a similar fashion, it needs to do more than it is doing at present. It has already achieved a great deal in a remarkably short time and, over time, it will become one of the more significant centers of power in the world. However, for the moment it needs to emulate China's speedy decision-making and still speedier implementation.

Chapter 2

The Changing
Investment Canvas

There is a large base of people in a number of countries in Asia who are well positioned on the road to prosperity. This base can be sliced into various demographics: a bulge segment of under-25-year-olds; a growing number of young dual-income families; and a growing mass-affluent segment—that is, people with increasing purchasing and investing power. In China, for example, by 2020 it is expected that nearly half of all families will be in the middle class and over three-quarters of these people will be found in urban centers.

This trend, though varying in intensity, rings true for other Asian growth centers as well. Even if the middle class across Asia grows at the GDP rate, at the minimum we are looking at doubling an already sizeable segment of the population every eight or nine years. Along with rising literacy levels and increasing disposable income the emergence of this class of people is one of the biggest investment catalysts in the world today.

This is not to suggest that the Asian middle class is one homogenous mass; quite the opposite, in fact, for there is no consistent definition of this Asian middle class. The middle class should ideally be defined as families that can afford to buy their own houses, an automobile, and all other perks that go with a middle-class lifestyle. By some other standards, the middle class comprises those families whose incomes are two-and-a-half times the national average. The World Bank for its part defines the middle class as households earning the equivalent of between US$10 and US$20 per day. Multinational companies and marketing organizations have struggled to understand the contours of the potential market and how much that market is willing to pay for goods and services. The fact that the potential middle-class market is large is beyond dispute; the real question is how large and what it means in purchasing power terms, especially for the more significant economies of India and China. Consulting firm McKinsey & Company defined China's lower-middle class as households earning between RMB25,001 and RMB40,000 per annum, and the upper-middle class as those households earning up to RMB100,000. According to McKinsey, the households earning RMB100,000 have an equivalent lifestyle to US households earning US$40,000 per annum. It further estimates that the lower-middle-class group will comprise 290 million people by 2011, with a total purchasing power equivalent to US$700 billion.

By all these assorted definitions the middle class in China is estimated to range between 80 million to 130 million people. The middle-class estimate for Asia (excluding Japan) is currently around 200–300 million people. This is a rapidly growing market, not only in size, but in per-capita disposable income, and represents the potential market for houses, personal loans, automobiles, mortgages, travel, higher education, entertainment, all forms of conspicuous consumption, and for financial assets. The World Bank estimates that by 2030, 93 percent of the world's middle class will be in developing nations (up from 56 percent in 2000) and two-thirds of that increase will be from China and India alone. Between now and 2030, China can be expected to add 350 million people and India close to 100 million people to the middle-class bracket.

The potential may well be even more significant. Overall, 40 percent of the world's population is found in India and China, but they have less than 10 percent of world's GDP; 58 percent of the world's people but less than 35 percent of its GDP (including the massive Japanese economy) are in Asia as a whole. But the fact that all the world's fastest-growing economies, companies, and sectors, and the largest blocks of emerging-market capitalization are in Asia underscores the tremendous potential for its share of world GDP to catch up. Some sectors did not even exist in an organized form a decade ago. Private education, for example, is now one of the most attractive from a strategic point of view to any global investor. Though many Asian nations have for years (and, in some cases, decades) created near double-digit GDP growth rates, Asia as a whole is still just one generation away from extreme poverty. Days of deprivation, war, poverty, scarcity, and other privations are still within the realm of collective consciousness. Other than those nations blessed with natural resources disproportionate to their populations, the common factors that pulled several Asian nations out of poverty and into the ranks of the developed or fast-developing nations is an increasingly educated population, state-directed support, the building of human and physical capital, and the rapid absorption of technology. The fact that stands above all others for most Asian families is that a solid education lies at the foundation of the Asian economic superstructure. In my view, private education is the sector that will give the greatest investment exposure to Asia's phenomenal rise. This sector has begun to experience explosive growth in several of the largest Asian countries but has barely been touched by investors and carries significant growth potential in the decades ahead. Global investors can expect more stories to unfold over the next few years as the growth potential of this industry drives existing players to seek out the capital markets.

Asia's "Learning Factories"

Having younger people as a large percentage of the population is an advantage when they are educated, opportunistic, and entrepreneurial. India, where over 50 percent of the population is under 25 years of age, has a larger percentage of younger people than any other nation. Education is both a key priority for governments and an opportunity for investors. So far, unlike in China and other parts of

Asia, the domestic Indian market for higher and technical education is operated almost exclusively through private or state-run colleges and university-affiliated or non-affiliated technical institutes. There are no commercial organizations with a national network of branches that provide technical education as is the trend in other parts of Asia. In fact, the opportunity that has grown exponentially in India consists almost entirely of university-entrance exam-prep classes such as those for the Indian Institutes of Technology (IIT) or private schools that provide exam coaching at the elementary and high-school level. The entrance-exam prep-course industry is dominated by local Indian brands that are closely associated with specific institutions or education streams. The larger and more reputable prep-course schools typically tend to have a single campus and function more like universities, with large bodies of students traveling and residing there during the preparatory period. The best-known and most highly regarded of these is Bansal Classes, which coaches around 17,000 students annually. Based in the northern city of Kota in Rajasthan state, it specializes in preparing high-school graduates for entry into the IITs. Such is its reputation that prep schools have now sprung up to guide students through the Bansal Classes entrance exam. Bansal Classes Private Ltd., the company that runs these sought-after prep courses, has estimated annual revenues of US$25 million and a track record spanning nearly two decades. Such has been its success that the city of Kota has now become the prep-course capital of India as far as technical entrance exams are concerned, with almost 150 prep schools catering to the breadth of university entrance exams including that of the All India Institute of Medical Sciences (AIIMS). Some of the larger private-education providers such as Resonance Institute coach close to 10,000 students annually. Though fragmented, the market size is enormous and growing very rapidly. For example, the IIT Joint Entrance Exam (JEE) has more than 300,000 students preparing for it every year, and they spend close to US$300 million annually on this one entrance exam alone. When other entrance exams such as the Common Admission Test, which is used as a unified entrance exam by the Indian Institutes of Management (IIM) and several others for medical and engineering courses, are factored in the spending pool enlarges to US$1.5–2 billion per annum. The overall size of the higher-education market in India is estimated at US$40 billion and is growing by 15 percent annually. As this pool grows, the demands on the established prep-school brands to develop a wider reach, establish branches, and even deliver learning content online could result in mergers or buyouts, especially considering that this is as close as one can get to a recession-proof industry.

Lotus Learning, another privately held Indian company, runs language laboratories in India, a very successful concept sold by the company to nearly 500 universities and schools across the country. This concept is great for a country where every student learns to read and write English from an early age but may not be comfortable speaking the language. Lotus Learning uses the proprietary system developed by Linguaphone Group Plc, the world's leading language-learning company.

Despite the presence of world-beating higher-education institutions, the overall quality of education in India, especially at the primary level, is below international standards and is one of the great paradoxes of India. Recent central government budgets have unveiled strong support for primary education, which will only deepen the opportunity for private education-service providers, and this space will remain one of the fastest-growing segments.

Despite the massive scale of the Indian education industry, it is China that is Asia's largest market for higher education across various disciplines. The tremendous desire of the Chinese to fit in with the rest of the world has led to an insatiable desire to learn the English language. The size of this market alone is now estimated at over US$2 billion annually and it is a long way yet from being mature. This has created a lot of opportunities for companies to set up language-training schools and to differentiate their offerings. The Walt Disney Company, one of the world's largest entertainment companies, has begun to capitalize on this trend in a great way, while building its core brand in China, as only Disney can. There are restrictions on the manner and extent to which Walt Disney and other entertainment and merchandising companies can go to advertise their brands and products, and the company has hit upon a novel way to introduce and anchor its brand within the Chinese consciousness. The company has now started teaching English to young Chinese students in major Chinese cities through branded Disney schools (which, incidentally, have become a novel way to introduce the Disney characters that are so well known to the rest of the world to Chinese children). The entire language-learning process is themed around Disney characters and movies. Disney currently has two schools in Shanghai, which it plans to increase to a total of six, and also plans to establish a school in Beijing.

Wall Street English, which was begun by the Wall Street Institute, is one of the leading English-language learning academies, with 35,000 adult students in 39 language schools in seven major Chinese cities. In April 2009, the company was bought by British media and education giant Pearson Plc, which also owns the Financial Times group and Penguin Publishing, for US$145 million, valuing it at more than twice its one-year forward revenues. That a seasoned player in the global education business was willing to pay this much for a fairly young business indicates the kind of growth expected from this niche market and the kind of serious players this niche industry is attracting. Wall Street English reported a 40 percent compounded growth in revenues between 2006 and 2008. The purchase of Wall Street English was Pearson's third purchase in China and made it the second-largest player in this market, with over US$100 million in revenues. The company has attributed its recent acquisition of language-education centers in China to the recognition within China of the importance of English-language skills to careers and earnings prospects and expects this trend to accelerate as the Chinese economy continues to integrate with the rest of the world.

The largest company in the Chinese education market is New Oriental Education Technology, which has its American Depository Receipt (ADR) listed in New York. The company offers child and adult English-language classes and Chinese and foreign university-entrance prep courses through 40 schools and 200 learning centers all over eastern China. It also operates 20 bookstores and distributes its proprietary software and materials to 5,000 other bookstores. It reported revenues of US$200 million in 2008, and revenues have grown by 36 percent annually for the past three years, while net income has gone up eight times, to US$49 million, in the same period. The ADR is richly valued at a 35 P/E multiple, yielding a valuation of ten times its sales and a market capitalization of US$2 billion as of May 2009. The rich valuation clearly reflects the diversified exposure, the market's expectation of its growth prospects and that of the Chinese education market. The other NYSE-listed ADR from this sector belongs to China Distance Education Holdings Ltd., which provides online certification in a number of professional disciplines. The company has seen volatility in net income in recent quarters but has been doubling revenues for the past couple of years. Despite a small revenue base, the ADR market capitalization is over US$200 million, with a P/E multiple of 50 times 2008 earnings. The huge valuations that these companies command has prompted a number of other Chinese education companies to seek an overseas listing and some 20 IPOs are expected between 2009 and 2012, which could reduce the novelty element and bring down valuations as the choices before investors increase.

This is but one trend that is driving the evolution of the education industry in China. A recent survey of Chinese students graduating from post-secondary institutions found that nearly 80 percent of them intend to study abroad. In reality, of the nearly 40 million students who graduate from secondary institutions every year barely 0.4 percent, or fewer than 150,000 students, actually go overseas for higher education. While foreign universities undoubtedly benefit from so many overseas Chinese students, this has created a huge demand for international-quality education in China from those who do not or cannot venture overseas.

The Chinese in general spend very heavily on education. According to China's Ministry of Education, the total annual expenditure on education by both the government and private citizens is around US$140 billion and is expected to reach US$175 billion by 2010. The size of the market is expected to grow by 20 percent until 2011. China Education Resources has developed and runs an education portal system geared toward teacher-training content. The Ministry of Education has teamed up with this portal to develop curriculum, and over 300 schools have already signed up for its content. The company has received applications from more than 800 schools, and the fact that it has a government ministry as a content-development partner makes it the obvious choice for schools to subscribe to its services, giving it a huge volume lead over any other rival.

China Educational Alliance Inc. is a mainstream education company based in China but it is traded on the US over-the-counter (OTC) market and provides educational services through its online portal, through an education center, and through its proprietary software. It caters to students from pre-school to middle school and also covers vocational training and continuing training, among other services. It also runs five English-language schools in China.

We've looked at the growth strategies of large global corporations seeking a piece of the education sector niche market and at examples of domestic Chinese companies catering to a mass market. There is still a third category of companies: ones that offer consultancy services to multinational corporations seeking to train their Chinese workforce in English. Yaxley Consulting is one such consulting firm. British in origin and currently privately held, it has been winning some excellent mandates from multinational firms in China, including Nokia and Indian wind-energy firm Suzlon Energy, among others.

South Korea too has a hyper-growth education market that has doubled in size twice since 2000 to be valued currently at between US$18–20 billion, but the market is fragmented. On a per-capita spending basis South Korea is the most valuable education market in the world, with tremendous potential for well-capitalized and reputable players willing to consolidate that market. The key to growth for educational companies in India and China too is consolidation in the vast but fragmented market populated by tens of thousands of players, most of whom are single-location players. The larger players with access to capital have proven how value-accretive their business models can be.

Asian Real Estate: More than Just Four Walls

Investors in real estate are, by definition, in for the long term and this is especially true in Asia, where strong gains accrue to those who choose the location of their assets well and are patient with them. While real estate as an asset class may boom in all kinds of places for all kinds of reasons, sustained runs are best supported by solid economic strength in a given region; that is, it is not enough to merely have falling interest rates and mortgage or refinancing rates to trigger a pick-up in real-estate prices, particularly in Asia where real estate is still largely financed with equity. There are several trends that are buffeting the Asian real-estate market, which has returned to a relative price appreciation after a very sharp dip during late 2008. Since the beginning of 2009 real-estate markets across Asia from China, Taiwan, Hong Kong, India, and Malaysia have seen a substantial pick-up in activity.

Figure 2.1 shows the property stock price indexes for Kuala Lumpur, Hong Kong, Jakarta, Taipei, and Shanghai from January 2008 to September 2009. With the exception of Jakarta, returns are still negative even though a recovery has occurred.

The key trends driving real-estate investment growth in both residential and commercial properties in Asia include a sizeable and growing segment of young people and their increasing mobility; the growth of urban areas; the rising standard of living; the growth in the number of double-income families; the growth of economic clusters; the growth of the service economy, including financial services, retailing, and tourism; and unprecedented growth in physical infrastructure linking coastal areas to the hinterland. Typically, real-estate purchases across most of Asia, particularly in China and India, are still underleveraged and the gradual widespread use of mortgage financing and the evolution of the securitization market will drive incremental real-estate investments and gains in coming years.

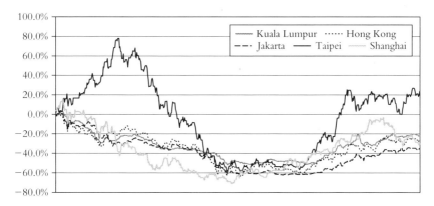

Figure 2.1 A comparative performance of selected Asian property markets
SOURCE: Bloomberg

The Urban Shift: Migration and the Creation of Mega-cities

Increasingly, Asian populations are shifting to urban areas in unprecedented numbers as jobs shift from rural to urban centers with growing
industrialization, and the significance of agriculture to GDP diminishes.
According to the United Nations Economic and Social Commission
for Asia and the Pacific (UNESCAP), urbanization is unfolding in
Asia at above the global average, though the spread is uneven across
Asian nations. The fastest rate of growth has occurred in Southeast and
Northeast Asia, where in the last two decades urban populations have
increased by two-thirds, to nearly 50 percent of the total population.
The rate of urbanization remains the fastest in Southeast Asia, with a
3.1 percent annual growth.

But this shift is not simply leading to the growth of sleepy towns
into bustling cities. Rather, it is creating a level of elite "mega-cities,"
which is driving an exponential growth in real-estate opportunities
across the region, as illustrated in Table 2.1.

In addition to this mega-city boom, changes are happening in traditional living concepts and the emergence of splinter families, especially in urban areas, is a key driver for the growth of a wide array
of products and services across Asia. Urbanization itself is a growing
middle-class phenomenon across Asia. Economists have predicted that
over two-thirds of all middle-class Asians will be living in urban areas
within the next decade. Demand for modern housing is growing

Table 2.1: The steady growth of Asian mega-cities and their global rankings

Rank in Asia (2007)	World Rank (2007)	City	Population (millions)			Average Annual Growth Rate (1975–2007)
			1975	2007	2025 (Expected)	
1	1	Tokyo	26.6	35.7	36.4	0.9%
2	4	Mumbai	7.1	19	26.4	3.1%
3	6	New Delhi	4.4	15.9	22.5	4.0%
4	7	Shanghai	7.3	15	19.4	2.2%
5	8	Kolkata	7.9	14.8	20.6	2.0%
6	9	Dhaka	2.2	13.5	22	5.6%

SOURCE: UNESCAP, Population Division

rapidly, as people demand higher standards than have been provided in the past. Rising income levels provide the means to achieve this. Demand for cars, vacations, entertainment, and all kinds of consumer needs all increase as discretionary spending power increases. Asia also has a high percentage of its urban population currently living in slums. UNESCAP estimates that the fast-developing Asian economies in Southeast Asia, China, and India have a range of 33–37 percent of their urban populations living in slums. Rehabilitation of these people and efforts to create more permanent solutions will also be a key driver for the local housing markets.

A key secondary trend is one where former joint families (extended families living together) break out of traditional structures, and younger families now seek their own living space. This trend is further accentuated as incomes rise along with the increase in double-income families, or families begin to seek second or holiday homes.

As Asian cities expand, companies engaged in construction, real-estate development, and management will be very significant beneficiaries, and smaller, highly competitive, and fast-growing companies may benefit exponentially. Hong Kong-listed company Agile Property Holdings Ltd. is a smaller developer of residential projects in Guangdong, one of China's fastest-growing provinces. This particular stock has outpaced returns from the Chinese real-estate sector for much of 2009 but has not yet tempered expectations that significant gains will accrue to it from sustained domestic economic growth. China Overseas Land and Investment Ltd. (COLI), a listed subsidiary of China Overseas Ltd., a state-owned real-estate investment company, is also a company to watch out for. As China and several other Asian countries begin to build out their entertainment centers and amusement parks, specialized contractors like COLI—which was involved with projects such as Hong Kong Disneyland and Space Mountain and has been short-listed for Shanghai Disneyland—could gain very significantly.

The Emergence of Asian Financial Centers

Financial capitals or emerging economic centers are always a good place to bet on: Shanghai, Mumbai, Abu Dhabi, Singapore, Seoul, and Jakarta.

Shanghai real estate as an investment destination is benefiting from multiple trends, and that city is enjoying almost constant stimulus from global events. In 2010 the World Expo will commence and last for six months, during which the city expects millions of visitors. This will be followed by the Shanghai Asian games. Similarly, the city of Tianjin, with its proximity to Beijing, is emerging as a rapidly growing economic city and already boasts a population of three million. It has the largest seaport in northern China, a large number of industries, and will be the site of China's third stock exchange. Property prices in Mumbai dipped during the worst of the global meltdown in 2008 but then were up 25 percent in the second half of 2009, while Chinese property prices have accelerated at a much faster pace. The Shanghai Property Index, representing Chinese property stocks, rose by 100 percent from January 2009 to August 2009, and returned nearly 70 percent through the worst of the downturn in the year to August 2009.

Real estate in Dubai has had a lot of appeal for global investors ever since investment norms were loosened to allow foreign investors in certain select areas of the city a few years ago. But without regulatory oversight, real-estate prices in Dubai quickly got out of hand and turned into a debt-fuelled speculative frenzy that produced a bubble that eventually burst in 2008−09. Subsequently there have been a number of criminal investigations into suspected large-scale embezzlements at the highest levels in leading real-estate and financial-services companies, which will continue to dent investor confidence in very important sectors. Once the dust settles in the Dubai real-estate market it could be a good time to look at that option again, given the city's position as one of the GCC region's two premier economic engines (Abu Dhabi being the other). Dubai houses the region's most dynamic financial market, major regional and global banks and brokerages, and media and technology companies. It is not surprising, given the tremendous soft skills and local and expatriate talent pool that Dubai has built, that the ruling families of the United Arab Emirates have committed to maintaining Dubai's prestige and put their money on the line, backing Dubai's large real-estate-linked loan obligations.

Abu Dhabi, on the other hand, has suffered no such leveraged crashes in real-estate prices and appears to be a far more solid investment opportunity. That city may eventually edge ahead of Dubai in both quality and scale of opportunity as the region's major investment destination. There are a number of very high-quality real-estate projects worth US$200 billion under way in Abu Dhabi. These cover the city's rapidly expanding tourist infrastructure as well its commercial and residential infrastructure that could be of interest to investors over the next few years. Abu Dhabi's vision is to turn itself into a financial and cultural center by 2030.

Singapore office, retail, and residential real estate has usually been treated as a proxy for the phenomenal growth in Asia. This is based on the city-state's close financial links with a number of major economies through free-trade agreements (FTA), and the fact that the its financial markets are a much-sought-after destination for companies and investors alike since many multinationals, global commercial and investment banks, and investment funds have their regional headquarters there. In addition, Singapore remains Asia's premier tourist and shopping destination, a fact that has consistently driven additions to retail space, especially at the high end of the market. The Singaporean office and retail real-estate sectors came into the 2008–09 global slowdown with a potential oversupply of built-up space, which may well last for the next couple of years. However, much of this capacity will be utilized given the fact that Singapore's population continues to grow by 2–3 percent a year, and its financial and economic involvement with Asia's rise is only increasing since it possesses one of the deepest and most sophisticated financial markets on the continent. The safest and best way to gain exposure to the Singaporean and some other East Asian real-estate markets is through the Real Estate Investment Trusts (REITs) listed on the SGX. The Singapore market has now become one of the most active for East Asian REITs outside of Japan, with several listings. One of the better SGX-listed REITs is Mapletree Logistics Trust (MLT). This is a good trust to evaluate because it holds commercial properties across multiple geographies: Japan, China, Korea, Malaysia, and Hong Kong. In the last quarter of 2008 and early 2009, falling occupancy rates in Hong Kong and China, where occupancy dropped to below 95 percent, were more than made up by sustained 100 percent occupancy rates in South Korea, Japan, and Malaysia. Equally importantly in the credit-challenged environment

Table 2.2:   Performance of selected REITs on the SET

REIT	Symbol	Total One-Year Return (%)	Assets Under Management (US$M)	Dividend Yield (%)
Samui Airport Property Fund	SPF	26.2	329	11.2
Quality Property Houses Fund	QHPF	25.0	262	9.6
CPN Leasehold Growth	CPNRF	13.1	339	9.8
Future Park Property Fund	FUTUREPF	9.0	149	10.9
Major Cineplex Lifestyle Lease	MJLF	7.0	82	11.0

SOURCE: Bloomberg

of 2008 and 2009, the trust was able to refinance its near-term debt maturities and raise capital for acquisitions of additional properties.

There are around 20 REITs listed on the Stock Exchange of Thailand (SET) and they still provide a very high and stable dividend yield. However, despite this, the Thai REITs in general suffer from low liquidity. Table 2.2 presents a list of a few better-performing REITs on the SET (ranked by total one-year returns).

Even though Singapore will be extremely hard to displace as a preferred investment destination or as a regional base for global corporations there is growing competition in the region for alternative investment destinations. As the capital of one of Asia's largest economies, Seoul is trying to build up its image as an emerging regional financial center that is driving significant development and real-estate opportunities. Seoul's importance will accelerate once it has completed the various FTAs and Asia Monetary Fund framework it is negotiating with several countries in the region. However, despite its many economic pluses, given the composition of the South Korean economy (heavy concentration in finance, electronics, and dependence on exports) it is also one of the most vulnerable to global shocks of the kind that we have seen in recent quarters.

The Emergence and Growth of Industrial Clusters

Financial capitals, while being very important real-estate investment destinations, are not the only trigger for a sustained appreciation in real-estate prices. Several cities across Asia are growing fast as a result of the development of rapidly growing industry clusters. These include IT and IT-enabled services in Bangalore and Manila; several manufacturing clusters in the Pearl River Delta in China; pharmaceuticals in Hyderabad; semiconductors in Hsinchu, Taiwan; and electronics and IT in the Cyber Jaya City and the Multimedia Super Corridor, Malaysia. The Malaysian real-estate sector has been one of the better-performing markets through the 2008–09 downtrend, with real-estate stock returns of 20 percent over the one-year period ending in August 2009.

The auto-component industry has developed several clusters in Asia. Component manufacturing drove development in areas around Chennai in Southern India and in specific centers in China. Yiwu City, in Zhejiang Province, is a commodity-trading cluster and contains the largest commodity market in the world. Over the last 14 years the city has been transformed from a small rural agricultural trading center into a major commodity market, with a population of almost two million and a well-regarded and heavily attended annual commodity trade fair. Some Asian construction companies have attained significant growth by focusing on rapidly expanding industrial clusters as they expanded. China Vanke Company Ltd. (2008 revenues of US$5.2 billion) has focused on the manufacturing clusters in the Pearl River Delta, building residential properties, and offering property-management services. It now focuses on all the mega and major Chinese cities such as Beijing, Shanghai, Shenzen, Guangzhou, Tianjin, Nanjing, Qingdao, and Chengdu, among others.

Port cities, too, do well when regional economies boom. Hong Kong is a great example of a real-estate market whose growth is closely correlated with its importance as a trading and regional money center and as the gateway to China. The dominant sectors in the Hong Kong economy are real estate and banks, with local venerable giants like Cheung Kong Holdings (with 2009 revenues of nearly US$2 billion and 18 percent five-year compound growth) and Sun Hang Kai

Development (US$5 billion in revenues and 12 percent five-year compound growth) figuring prominently. There are other, faster-growing names such as China Resources Land, with US$1.2 billion in revenues and a 49 percent five-year compound growth in revenues and 92 percent CAGR in net income. Hong Kong property stocks have not produced a negative return in any year for the past two decades and have produced an average annual return of 7–8 percent over this period. Shanghai is in that same position now. However, in several parts of Asia it makes sense to keep investments in key regional markets and not spread them around—simply because general economic growth may be accelerating and pushing up prices everywhere. Very often, peripheral markets in smaller cities and towns offer superlative returns but cannot sustain these since the buying impetus tends to be local and often speculative.

Tourism as a Driver for Asian Real Estate

Other emerging investment destinations are cities such as Bangkok, Thailand; Muscat (capital of the Sultanate of Oman); and Shenzen, China, which are largely driven by tourism. Thailand has focused on improving its basic tourist infrastructure, especially airports and hotels, and Bangkok has been a major beneficiary. The Thai real-estate market has rewarded investors well in the past several years but has been hit, first, by the political instability of the last couple of years and, more recently, by the global financial crisis. However, the Thai construction companies have held on operationally (though not necessarily to their market values) through these crises and deserve a closer look. These companies learned a brutal lesson during the 1997–98 Asian currency crisis when Thailand, along with the Philippines, Indonesia, and South Korea, was at the epicenter of that meltdown and the construction sector was decimated. The trigger for that crisis in Thailand was the speculative real-estate bubble built up in Thai tourist resorts that were financed with short-term foreign-exchange loans. Having learned their lesson from that experience Thai companies have since focused only on the higher end of the market, with premium projects being sold to well-heeled Thai and foreign nationals for cash. A very small percentage of Thai real estate now is leveraged. We will examine the long-term drivers for these companies a little later, when we discuss tourism in Asia and its impact on real estate.

Tourism is fueling real-estate growth in the Middle East, and it is not just regular tourist infrastructure such as hotels rooms, convention centers, airports, and recreational centers that are being added in large quantities. A rather grand vision of a region transformed into the world's tourist hub and cultural playground is being translated into mega real-estate investments. Abu Dhabi more than any of the other oil-rich sheikhdoms is completely reinventing itself from an oil-producing desert into an economically diversified cultural oasis potentially fueled by tourism, much like the great tourist resort centers of the world, such as Bali, Phuket, Puerto Rico, Mexico, and Costa Rica, but with a uniquely Arabian influence and perspective. The center-piece of its extravagant reinvention is a US$27 billion investment in a cultural center spanning an entire island (the "Island of Happiness") spread over 27 square km, designed and developed by some of the world's leading architects. Among the cultural pieces planned are the Louvre Abu Dhabi, the first Louvre Museum outside of Paris; the Guggenheim Abu Dhabi; a national museum of contemporary arts; a maritime museum; and a performing-arts center. In addition, there will be nine luxury hotels, an 18-hole golf course, a world-class concert hall, and two 10-lane highways connecting the island to the Abu Dhabi mainland.

The Tourism Development and Investment Company (TDIC), which is currently owned by the UAE government, is the company tasked with completion of each of the specific projects that make up the world's largest cultural center. The company has entered into several specific joint ventures. A number of global hotel chains such as Fairmont and Starwood are involved with projects there and for some it marks their first entry into the Middle East. The company is responsible for carrying out Abu Dhabi's entire tourism development efforts, which include several large tourism-related residential, leisure, hospitality, and commercial projects. The strenuous efforts to create state-of-the-art tourist infrastructure on such an unprecedented scale also offer opportunities for foreign and domestic investors to buy pieces of several residential projects or purchase land on the island and develop their properties according to specifications in the master development plan. The drawback is that only investors from the Gulf Cooperation Council nations can own land here, whereas all other investors will be leased land for periods of 50 to 99 years. There is currently no indication that the restrictive covenants governing land rights for foreign investors will change any time soon. It is not surprising therefore, that despite the vision of the government and tremendous potential of these projects, UAE real estate (especially in Dubai) has attracted the more speculative elements, rather than stable long-term owners/investors. For the vast majority of global investors it might be easier and less risky to participate in the stocks of construction companies and wait for names like TDIC to go public than to take direct exposure to real estate. The hope is that as Abu Dhabi expands into a regional and global financial hub its cultural appeal, backed by massive infrastructure, will also blossom, leading to an influx of people who will invest in property, take up residence, and drive the domestic economy.

Despite the competition and a question mark over the length of time needed for Dubai's resurgence, that city will benefit since all the material suppliers, investors, media companies, and a talent pool of expatriates are based there and will be crucial to Abu Dhabi's quest to become a global city.

Qatar, a country with the second-highest per-capita income in the world (at US$103,000), is investing US$17 billion in its own tourism industry over a five-year period, most of which is concentrated in the capital city, Doha. Saudi Arabia is targeting US$19 billion in revenue from tourism over the next five years. This is no pipe dream. Dubai generates the third-highest average room rates in the world, at US$300, according to consulting firm Deloitte, while it generated the second-highest revenues per available room (revPAR) in 2008, at US$237. Abu Dhabi's revPAR increased by 46 percent during 2008, justifying the numerous hotel projects in that city-state. Muscat gained 31 percent in revPAR in 2008. According to the World Tourism Organization (UNWTO) there were 924 million tourist arrivals in 2008, of which the Middle East's share was around 5 percent. The UNWTO now expects that by 2020 this region will see close to 70 million arrivals, a growth of nearly 7 percent per annum over the 38 million who came in 2006. Expected growth in tourism has driven the expansion of hotel capacity in this region, especially of the super-luxury variety, and is a clear driver for infrastructure addition in much of the rest of Asia too.

East Asian countries provide the biggest source of tourists both within and outside Asia. In South Korea, for example, 75 percent of foreign tourists come from Japan, Hong Kong, Taiwan, and China. China will soon take over from Japan as the biggest source of tourists to the rest of the world. But as China grows and as the fascination with it grows too, there will be a powerful pull factor for inbound tourism as well. Even global entertainment giants have already jumped in, with Disney contemplating a US$4 billion investment in a Disneyland theme park in Shanghai.

Needless to say, the hospitality sector has been the recipient of massive doses of investments, ranging from super-luxury hotels in the Middle East catering to upscale travelers, to business hotels in India, to spas and casinos catering to waves of Chinese tourists in East Asia. There is also a clear link between the evolution of gaming in Asia and the boom in regional tourism. According to the World Tourism Organization, China is likely to produce 100 million outbound visitors every year by 2020. The impact of this on global tourism revenues will be significant considering that the Chinese already spend about 1.5 percent of their GDP as tourists overseas.

Gaming and Casinos: Chinese Roulette

Macau has become Asia's answer to Las Vegas, with some of the biggest Las Vegas names now setting up ambitious projects in this tiny South China Sea island. In fact, as of 2006 Macau is bigger than Las Vegas in gaming revenue terms. Asia's immense passion for gambling coupled with a lifting of travel restrictions on mainland Chinese by the Chinese government has led to an exponential increase in tourist traffic from the mainland to Macau. The Chinese government also opened the tourism and gaming sector to competition in 2003 and this in turn has led to a spurt in investment activity in the hospitality sector that is pretty much unrivalled. All these factors pushed Macau's GDP growth to 15 percent for 2008. If it were an independent nation, its GDP growth would be nothing short of astounding.

The multi-billion-dollar investment effort by the Las Vegas Sands Corporation in Macau (through the Sands Macau Ltd., which is working on its IPO at the time of writing) is reflective of how important the Far East has become to global hospitality companies. The Venetian Macau, its flagship hotel and the single largest hotel in Asia, cost nearly US$2.5 billion and opened its doors in late 2007, just as the global financial markets were beginning to weaken. Las Vegas Sands, though, has been hit very hard by the global credit squeeze (the company's credit quality has been below investment grade since before the global financial crisis began) and slowdown, and ultimately may not achieve the depth of presence it wants to develop in Asia. Nevertheless, it does reflect the potential before the tourism and gambling industries in Asia, even though Macau itself looks overbuilt in the near term (when projects by other developers are taken into account).

Even conservative Singapore, which has traditionally focused on finance and trade and where real estate has traditionally been associated with office and residential properties, is getting into the new-age tourist game with the construction of new hotels and casinos, with an eye on the ever-increasing number of visitors from China. Genting Berhad, Asia's biggest publicly traded casino operator (with listed subsidiaries in Singapore, Malaysia, and the US), has built a US$4 billion casino on Singapore's Sentosa Island that will be fully operational in 2010. Its Malaysian subsidiary company, Genting Malaysia Berhad, is a monopoly casino operator in that country.

However, Chinese domestic tourism is also likely to grow since Chinese nationals are now once again permitted to visit Buddhist shrines and ancient temples, a practice that had been prohibited during the communist era. The Chinese have a very interesting and integrated approach to tourism, much like they have toward their important industries. Local governments have recognized that combining the attractions of the remarkable natural beauty and historical landmarks with the significant industrial achievements of their communities makes for a unique tourism opportunity. The city of Xi'an (China's capital during several periods of imperial rule and made famous by the discovery of thousands of life-size terracotta warriors), for example, has pooled its resources with one of its outlying districts to offer aerial tours of sites of natural beauty and historical significance. Along with developing new tourist ventures the local government also plans to open the manufacturing facilities of one of the country's leading aircraft manufacturers, the Xi'an Aircraft Industries Group, to tourists.

According to the World Travel and Tourism Council, tourism contributes some 140 million jobs in the Asia-Pacific region, accounting for roughly 9 percent of employment. In China, 10 percent of the workforce is engaged in tourism and related activities (putting it on an equal footing with both Thailand and the Philippines), as compared to 5.4 percent for India. Between 1996 and 2006 the Asia-Pacific region's share of the tourist dollar increased from 16 percent to nearly 25 percent, representing US$160 billion annually in revenues (see Table 2.3). Also, the region's share of tourist arrivals increased from 17 percent to 27 percent, driven largely by gains in India and China, and these figures are set to increase exponentially with the lowering of travel barriers for Asians within Asia and the effort to woo travelers from across the world too.

India is being increasingly touted as the next great tourist destination after China. It has a great deal to offer in the way of varied cultural

Table 2.3: Tourism revenues as a proportion of GDP among the major tourist nations

Country/Region	Revenues as a % of GDP
Malaysia	6.7%
Thailand	6.5%
Singapore	5.2%
Philippines	3.0%
Indonesia	1.2%
South East Asia	3.7%
Hong Kong	6.1%
China	1.2%
India	1.0%
South Korea	0.7%
Japan	0.2%
Europe	2.2%
North America	0.7%

SOURCE: World Trade Organization

sites and stunning natural beauty. The Indian government's efforts to promote the nation's tourist locations worldwide through slick advertising campaigns have paid off, with tourism growing by 15–16 percent annually. Along with this has come significant growth for tour operators such as Thomas Cook India, which recorded 2008 revenues of US$3.1 billion and a revenue compounded annual growth rate (CAGR) of 25 percent. Another top tour operator is Cox and Kings, which is unlisted at the moment and has been in India for nearly 100 years. India has some strong domestic hotel chains such as Indian Hotels, owners of the Taj Group of Hotels, and EI Hotels, owners of the Oberoi chain, that have begun to expand overseas as well with some prime properties in Asia, Europe, and the US. Indian Hotels remains one of the better-managed hotel chains in the world, and the stock has returned an annualized 20 percent over the last two decades, outpacing the returns of Mumbai's BSE Sensex index over the same period.

Thailand's Unique Real-Estate Market

Thailand offers very different investment opportunities, either directly in its tourist resorts or by taking exposure to its leading real-estate companies. There has always been foreign-investor demand for high-end properties in Thai resort towns since foreigners typically purchase condominiums and rent them out. There is also a demand for luxury villas in Phuket and Pattaya, which come with property-management services sometimes offered by five-star hotels.

The Setprop Index, representing 50 Thai property stocks, has outperformed both the Thai stock market and most other regional and global markets since bottoming out in October 2008 (see Figure 2.2).

Thai real-estate projects remained on track despite the severity of the price crash in the housing market, with seemingly minimal project disruptions—at least in the case of the leading and better-capitalized developers such as Sansiri. Sansiri is a 25-year-old company, with revenues of US$450 million. The company was one of the first to restructure and de-leverage in 2000, in the aftermath of the 1997–98 crisis. Sansiri now develops properties for sale and rent and offers property-management and hospitality services, running boutique hotels and an award-winning spa. The US hospitality chain Starwood Group is a partner to Sansiri. Land & Houses Public Co., the largest

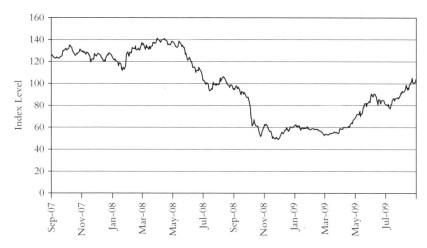

Figure 2.2   Thai property stocks index

and most-profitable Thai construction company, with US$470 million in revenues, brings strong exposure to the condominium market as well as hospitals, and the government of Singapore has a 12.6 percent stake. Raimon Land Co., one of the largest developers in Thailand's tourist capital, Pattaya, is the other strong property player. The Thai resort market, especially in Pattaya, has remained strong largely due to purchases made by Russian, Northern European, East Asian, and Middle Eastern investors. Most developers have resisted cutting prices as of the second quarter of 2009, but may not be able to do so for long if the political instability in Thailand continues and demand from foreign buyers weakens. However, despite the combination of lukewarm international investor sentiment for Thai property and continuing building supply, prices of high-end property (which is where foreign investors typically congregate) have actually increased. Rentals in those properties have also remained strong. In light of the recent earnings gains for Thai real-estate companies there may be a good opportunity for investors to pick up solid companies in this environment of political instability given the severe drop in share prices over 2008 and 2009.

Hospitality and tourism are key growth areas for Asia as a whole, but it is in the Middle East that these sectors and associated developments are taken most seriously. Similar trends are driving the considerable opportunity in the Middle Eastern hospitality sector.

Besides luxury hotels, airlines such as Arabian Air and Jazeera are good examples of growth prospects as travel to and within the region increases. While these companies are currently privately held, with rapid development and the increasing ability of the regional stock markets to intermediate, it is only a matter of time before they attempt to raise capital from the public, and investors should be prepared for this.

Some good plays on the Indian real-estate scene are DLF and Unitech. Several Indian real-estate companies listed on London's AIM market after a significant bout of capital-raising in the early to mid-2000s, though few are of genuine investment quality. One potentially interesting player (though more for pedigree than performance) is Indiabulls Properties Investment Trust, India's first and, so far, only REIT (listed on the Singapore Stock Exchange). This trust is partly backed by Lakshmi Mittal, CEO of steel giant Arcelor Mittal, and is a part of India's fourth-largest real-estate group. The REIT, which is largely equity funded (leverage of under 10 percent), owns a minority stake in two recently completed office buildings in Mumbai but is as yet unprofitable. At the time of writing the trust traded at less than 40 percent its net asset value (NAV). Even though the timing of Indiabull's floating a REIT in Singapore could not have been worse (summer of 2008) and its returns to investors have been dismal, other Indian property developers (the better-capitalized and reputable ones) are also known to be looking at SGX REITs as an option and are awaiting improved market conditions.

Yatra Capital is a Euronext-listed Indian real-estate fund that is focused on investing in property in the smaller towns and cities, which are usually labeled tier I and tier II cities. The fund returned 135 percent to investors in the first eight months of 2009. Phoenix Mills Ltd., on the other hand, focuses entirely on tier I cities such as Mumbai, New Delhi, Chennai, and Bangalore. The company has a strong bank of properties under development in Mumbai, one of the strongest real-estate markets in India. The stock suffered a 90 percent drop during 2008 but has appreciated three times from its 2008 low during the early part of 2009.

Chinese property-development companies too are ones to watch as the domestic economy picks up and investment in private housing increases. Housing will be an area of policy focus and government backing since that is the new engine for Chinese growth.

Poly Real Estate Group, which is a listed but essentially state-owned company, is one of the larger and better-capitalized Chinese real-estate companies. The company's business segments range from property development, interior design, and relocation of buildings to earthworks and road building. It has built a strong growth track record, and in 2008–09 revenue growth stood at 92 percent. For the first half of 2009–10 the company reported sales growth of 165 percent. It generated a return on equity of 18 percent against the average RoE of other real-estate companies of 10 percent. There are other smaller but profitable companies such as China Enterprise Company Ltd. and the Beijing Capital Company.

Real-estate business is renowned for being terribly cyclical, and real-estate companies are notorious for going bankrupt. However, one of the important results of the Asian real-estate and currency crisis of 1997–98 was the maturing of companies in East Asia. The Middle Eastern real-estate companies, even giant companies such as Emmar in Dubai, are undergoing significant changes of their own. Emmar was a product of Dubai's carnival of speculative frenzy and is now paying the price for over-building and aggressive financing. Obviously, there are very few companies that can weather both a depressed market and a heavy debt load.

Retailing: "We Can Do It, You Can Learn"

This could very likely be Home Depot's advertising tag line in China, where the US retailing giant is targeting its future expansion. In the US, where the do-it-yourself (DIY) market is the cornerstone of the economics of home-improvement stores such as Home Depot and Lowe's, in Asia their approach will be the exact opposite: they will need to offer complete installation services at no extra cost if they are to wean customers away from the unorganized, semi-skilled handymen who currently dominate the market. While the DIY home-improvement concept may not really catch on in other parts of Asia either, there is enough of a growth market for Home Depot to target Asia in a fairly big way, with 14 stores to be opened in China alone.

Other retailing segments have certainly picked up considerably. For example, Hengdeli Holdings Ltd. (formerly known as Xinyu Hengdeli Holdings Ltd.), a high-end retailer of watches, has more than 200 stores spread over China, Hong Kong, and Taiwan. The company is partly owned by Swatch Group AG of Switzerland, the world's largest watch maker, and by LVMH Moët Hennessy Luis Vuitton SA, the world's largest luxury brand. In anticipation of the growing demand for luxury goods in the Greater China region, the company expects to have 250 stores in operation by the end of 2009 and a total of 280 stores by 2010. The stock has produced an annual return of 44 percent between 2005 and 2009.

Another high-end retailer operating successfully in China and Hong Kong is Ports Design Ltd. Like Hengdeli the Port Design stock has returned 42 percent annual returns from 2004 until 2009. The Hong Kong and Taiwanese exchanges have a wide variety of listed specialty and multi-line retailers as well as companies that are fully exposed to the Chinese consumer. Anta Sports Products Ltd. produces sports footwear and apparel for the general retail and professional sports markets in China. The company has the entire range of functions, from design and development to manufacturing and marketing. Its brands are very popular in China and it has reported 71 percent compound revenue growth for the past five years. It is quite profitable and has a formidable competitive advantage in a market notorious for copycat designs and cheap products. The respective performances of other retail companies are set out in Table 2.4.

Anchored by giant supermarkets or retail brands, in India the entire retailing format is undergoing a rapid evolution driven by the proliferation of malls, the emergence of strong retail brands, and the desire for a more upscale Westernized shopping experience. Very often, buying into retailers at a reasonably early stage of their growth is a great way to also participate in the development of real estate. The promoter of India's Big Bazaar department store once said that he spends more time with realtors picking out his locations and locking in long-term lease rates than on any other aspect of his business. Indian retailers are still in their early stages, and not all the big players are consistently profitable yet.

China is a good example for India to follow. Where just a few years ago retailing in the urban areas of China was completely dominated by

Table 2.4: Asian retailers: Strong growth across the board

Company	Product	2008 Revenue	Revenue (5-Year CAGR)	Net Income (5-Year CAGR)	Current Market Cap (Oct 2009)	RoE 5-Year Average
Daphne International	Manufacturer and retailer of footwear	US$680 million	24%	36%	US$1.5 billion	35%
Ports Design	Garment & accessories manufacturer and retailer	US$214 million	16%	26%	US$1.5 billion	32%
Wumart	Supermarkets in Beijing	US$1,260 million	28%	35%	US$2.1 billion	15%
Anta Sports	Professional footwear and apparel	US$665 million	71%	43%	US$3.2 billion	32%
Belle International	Women's footwear retailer	US$2,560 million	83%	91%	US$9.0 billion	28%
Shufersal Ltd.	Grocery store chains in Israel	US$3,060 million	12.5%	NA	US$1.2 billion	10.6%
Blue Square	Supermarkets and specialty stores in Israel	US$2,080 million	8%	NA	US$500 million	13%

Source: Bloomberg

single small stores, it has been completely transformed into a large-store format dominated by brands, and Wal-Mart and Carrefour have become top players. Wal-Mart is looking actively at its strategy in India (where it has a joint venture with the Bharti Group) and recent announcements indicate that it has switched tactics from a retail focus to a wholesale focus. Wal-Mart's potential entry into retailing led to massive protests from small retailers across the country, which probably nudged the company into a more inclusive format. This wholesale or cash-and-carry format will be a boon for retailers since they can now purchase directly from a giant company that can make the supply-chain investments and provide the goods they need for their business in a more cost-effective manner.

Asia's Story on Wheels

Following real estate, the automobile industry is the fulcrum of growth in Asia, and it is urbanization that drives automobile sales. The bulk of the developing world's auto sales are in urban areas; for example, 10 percent of the cars in China are in Beijing alone, though that city has just 1 percent of the country's population. While auto sales have slowed down during the worst of the global economic crisis, it remains an expanding market, and as of the first quarter of 2009 China has overtaken the US as the world's largest automobile market, producing more than a million cars a month.

Other Asian auto manufacturers have made the news: India's Tata Motors for innovative new models and China's Geely Automobile Holdings for some serious upscaling and capacity expansion. Geely Automobile Holdings is China's largest independent car manufacturer (the largest manufacturer is Shanghai Auto, which also has the largest market capitalization).

The five largest car markets in Asia are Japan, South Korea, China, India, and Thailand, but the distribution across nations by cars per thousand people is also diverse, ranging from 12 for India to 265 for Japan. The figure for India is misleading because it only includes automobiles, whereas motorcycles are a far more popular form of transportation, and India is the world's second-largest market for motorcycles.

Fast-growing automobile markets are a phenomenon across Asia, even in economies such as Vietnam, where the market for autos is growing by 12–15 percent per annum and is well in excess of its GDP growth rate. In China, the key driver of the auto market is the increasing affordability in all segments of Chinese society, especially for low- and medium-priced cars. Nearly 95 percent of urban households and 90 percent of rural households can afford a low-priced car and these figures are expected to be applied to medium- and high-priced cars over the next decade. Compared to the Chinese auto market, India, on the other hand, is still behind in size. However, the growth and sophistication of its auto segment has been no less pulsating. India has a very well-developed market for small-capacity motorcycles and scooters, producing several million a year. The market has evolved with domestic innovation focusing on robust but simple models providing superior fuel efficiency. India's auto strategy has been to wean buyers away from two-wheelers or used cars, while the strategy of two-wheeler manufacturers has been to move buyers up the value chain to more powerful motorcycles or more stylish scooters where profit margins are better. India is now home to the world's largest motorcycle manufacturers, Hero Honda and Bajaj Auto, which compete fiercely for market share in India and are now expanding overseas, largely within Asia. Iconic brands such as Harley Davidson and BMW are set to launch their high-end bikes in India in 2010.

The automotive sectors in the world's two largest emerging economies could not be more different. While China has the larger production numbers and better scale of operations, its domestic auto-production capability, with more than a hundred local manufacturers, is completely disjointed. This is clearly unsustainable, and there will likely be a consolidation soon. Given the fact that an FTA between Korea, Japan, and China is inevitable, the Chinese domestic automotive sector will undoubtedly suffer. It is the larger companies which have a better chance of succeeding, especially those with existing relationships with Japanese or Korean manufacturers.

Chinese auto makers operate under unique arrangements where they partner with more than one foreign manufacturer while attempting to manufacture cars on their own. They also typically manufacture critical assemblies through subsidiary companies, which, in turn, have joint ventures with foreign technology partners. Few have reached a point where they will be commercially viable on their own in the long run.

India, by comparison, has a very focused and consolidated auto sector, with two domestic car manufacturers competing with half a dozen large global players. It is the low-end models that have mass appeal in India, and Suzuki Motors has dominated that space since the 1980s, though Tata Motors has created a successful presence in that segment in under 10 years of manufacturing passenger cars. Indian manufacturers, like their compatriots in other industries, enjoy very significant returns on capital and in a capital-constrained environment are well positioned to deliver value. Bajaj Auto and Hero Honda enjoy high capital returns.

The largest manufacturer of passenger cars in China by volume is SAIC Motors (formerly Shanghai Automotive Company), which produces almost two million passenger and commercial vehicles a year. (GM, with an annual volume of two million vehicles, is the largest foreign manufacturer, and Geely Auto is the largest private-sector car maker—see Table 2.5.) Like Tata Motors and Suzuki before it, SAIC too has targeted the mini-car market and is now the largest producer of mini-cars in China. However, it has yet to reverse the multi-year trend in losses and, in any case, foreign investors cannot access the stock since it is an A-share and thus available only to domestic investors.

Most of the global car manufacturers came to these markets with many of the models that had been successful in other markets but have realized that the real mass market exists in low-priced small cars. Both Ford Motors and GM Chevrolet are now preparing to launch mini cars of their own in India. Chevrolet launched its second small car in India in 2009, the engine for which will also be manufactured there by the last quarter of 2010. For its part, Ford Motors will launch the Magna Electric car in India by 2011. Similarly, Renault and Nissan, which have combined their business strategy in India, have scrapped most plans for adding new models with the exception of what they have termed an ultra-low-cost car to be rolled out in 2011 in collaboration with Bajaj Auto.

It is not just Indian or Chinese car makers or auto-parts suppliers that can exploit the fast-growing markets here. Canada's Magna International, the largest auto-parts group in the world, is in the process of greatly expanding its manufacturing and design and development

Table 2.5: A cross-section of Chinese auto companies listed in Hong Kong and available to foreign investors

Company	Production	Current Revenue	5-Year Revenue Growth	5-Year Average Net Income Growth	Current Market Cap (Oct 2009)	RoE 5-Year Average
Geely Automobile	Passenger cars	US$617 million	NA	70.1%	US$2.5 billion	19.2%
BYD*	Battery powered automobiles, autos, batteries, bicycles	US$3.85 billion	38%	3.4%	US$23.9 billion	18.7%
Dongfeng Group	Light trucks, cars, diesel engines	US$10.2 billion	14.9%	3.9%	US$10.1 billion	20.9%
Great Wall Motors	Pick-up trucks, SUVs	US$1.2 billion	25.1%	11.1%	US$1.1 billion	14.2%
Weichai Power Equipment	Diesel engines	US$4.7 billion	39.5%	43.7%	US$6.7 billion	26.5%
FAW Car Co	Cars and auto parts	US$2.8 billion	16.2%	28.2%	US$4.5 billion	9.1%
SAIC Motors	Cars and auto parts	US$15.1 billion	69.5%	(10%)	US$20.3 billion	9.9%
Tianjin FAW Xiali Auto	Mini cars	US$1 billion	7.2%	NA	US$2.4 billion	5.2%

SOURCE: Bloomberg
*32% percent of BYD's revenues come from automobiles; the remainder comes from mobile handset components and batteries

capability in India, not just for its Indian operations but also to support its global business.

Amtek Auto Ltd., the Indian company that has been selected to develop and supply power trains for the car, has a joint venture with Magna Powertrain. Amtek Auto in turn is one of the largest auto-component manufacturers in India. The company has a strong track record of profitability, and currently 50 percent of its equity is held by foreign institutional investors (FIIs).

India has emerged as a global hub for the manufacture of auto components (see Table 2.6) and is home to one of the world's largest foundries: Bharat Forge Ltd. The industry's competitiveness was born out of the auto boom of the 1990s, where numerous joint ventures were set up and huge capacities built. This led to manufacturing overcapacity and Indian companies were forced to differentiate and compete overseas by building top-quality products and delivery systems that led to global manufacturers outsourcing from them in a very big way.

Based on the investment pattern of global auto manufacturers and component manufacturers, the Indian and Chinese auto sectors are expected to contribute to most of the growth in automotive volumes, both in vehicles and components, especially since the number of models available to consumers and the number of car manufacturers targeting Asia is expected to rise significantly. A number of companies are already implementing significant expansion of scale in anticipation of that growth.

Both countries will continue to emerge as dominant markets for planes, trains, and automobiles.

The Art World: Asia's Next Investment Horizon

As nations become wealthier, the wealthy in those nations tend to take a keen interest in their own and the world's cultural heritage. Abu Dhabi's decision to invest US$27 billion in a gigantic cultural complex on a specially developed island is a staggering manifestation of this sentiment. This development will go a long way to shifting the center of gravity of the global art world to Asia. While the Middle East is clearly

Table 2.6: A cross-section of leading Indian auto and component manufacturers

Company	Production	Revenue FY 08-09 (US$)	5-Year Revenue Growth	5-Year Average Net Income Growth	Current Market Cap (Oct 2009)	RoE 5-Year Average
Hero Honda	Motorcycles	$2.7 billion	10.7%	9.6%	$6.8 billion	45.7%
Ashok Leyland	Trucks	$1.3 billion	7.4%	(7%)	$1.3 billion	33.7%
Mahindra & Mahindra	SUVs, tractors	$4.2 billion	19.9%	15.6%	$5.6 billion	31.3%
Bosch Ltd.*	Fuel-injection systems, filters, spark plugs, wipers	$1.1 billion	14.3%	11.1%	$2.9 billion	27.6%
Bajaj Auto	Motorcycles, scooters	$1.8 billion	8.1%	(7.7%)	$4.6 billion	22.9%
Maruti Suzuki	Cars	$4.5 billion	13.5%	6.9%	$9.4 billion	21.5%
Amtek Auto	Engine, transmission and suspension systems	$1.2 billion	42.6%	43.5%	$0.6 billion	21.1%
Tata Motors	Cars, SUVs, trucks	$16.4 billion	31.1%	NA	$6.0 billion	18.1%
Apollo Tyres	Automotive tyres	$1.09 billion	17.5%	17.7%	$0.6 billion	15.2%
Bharat Forge	Steel forgings & machined components	$1.2 billion	19.4%	(22%)	$1.3 billion	18.1%

SOURCE: Bloomberg
*The German Bosch Group has six subsidiaries in India and 18,000 employees including a company (Bosch Ltd.) publicly listed in India.

emerging both as a major destination of art and as a source of nouveau art collectors, real market action has already ignited in China, which has a sizeable and rapidly developing art market, and in India, which has unexpectedly turned out to be a growing and valuable art market.

When a leading Indian industrialist purchased at auction a rare sword used by a seventeenth-century Indian king, it set the art world abuzz for two reasons: first, it set a new price standard for Indian artifacts, and second, it marked a major entry of a new class of buyers in the global art scene.

What these examples underscore is an interesting and growing investment option. In India, for example, artwork by contemporary masters has begun to produce astonishing long-term returns. Using auction prices as a benchmark and by observing some private deals (which may not be the best indicator of returns) 25-year compounded returns typically range from 27 percent to 30 percent per annum. Returns from other artists who are only just attaining renown have also been no-less spectacular, typically showing annual compound returns over a 15–20-year period ranging from 20–25 percent. The Indian market is currently valued at US$400 million, though these are only rough estimates. Compare this with a global art market size of US$60 billion and you can get a sense of the growth potential. By some estimates within the art-fund management community, the Indian art market should be worth around US$1 billion within a couple of years. Artwork is still within reach of more investors in India than anywhere else simply because many artists still sell their works fairly cheaply and those looking to build a diversified exposure to Asia may consider a whole new canvas, so to speak. A number of local art houses with a good understanding of the local and global art scene have sprung up in the last five to seven years, and the big-name global art houses too have expanded their presence in India, which will undoubtedly help the market become better organized. Increasingly, deals are being done through auctions to improve transparency, since allegations of price-rigging by several art dealers have emerged in recent months. The Securities and Exchange Board of India (SEBI), the Indian market regulator, has now brought art funds under its purview. Art funds have begun to make their presence felt, though these typically have a higher initial investment amount, which could be upward of US$50,000.

By participating in these funds, investors will have an opportunity to own a pool of art—usually paintings or sculptures—rather than individual works of art.

A key driver of emerging art value in India is the growing recognition of talent within India by external buyers. Until recently, the vast majority of Indian art works at international auctions have been purchased by wealthy non-resident Indians. This is changing slowly as more global collectors begin to take note of Indian art. The Fine Art Group of the UK, one of the world's first and its largest international art-fund management company, has established the Indian Fine Art Fund, a US$15–25 million fund raised entirely outside of India. The group also has a Chinese Fine Art Fund and a Middle Eastern Fine Art Fund. Gradually, there is a growing worldwide acceptance of Indian artists, as there has been of Chinese and other Asian artists. Works by Indian masters have begun to command increasingly higher prices at international auctions, in many cases topping US$1 million. Of the other art funds active in India, the Osian Art Fund, launched in 2006, is the largest. Other big names include the Kotak Mahindra Bank's Art Fund, the Yatra Fund, Crayon Capital Fund, and a US$25 million art fund from ICICI Bank. Very typically these are five-year, closed-ended funds that look to distribute capital gains at the end of the holding period.

While art investing may be for the fast-growing wealthy classes in India, China, and the Middle East, it is in other lifestyle sectors that the changes in mass-market attitudes are being felt.

Media, Entertainment, and Lifestyle Change

Lifestyle changes, a more youthful populace, and, more importantly, the availability of larger disposable income have all been good news for Hollywood, for Bollywood, and for other regional movie and television industries. Local-language programming has seen a massive increase in volume and revenues since the mid-1990s. There has been an increase in the number and depth of companies, from listed movie makers and serial producers, to cable and TV channel owners, especially in the Indian marketplace. The Indian TV market has grown from virtually zero in the late 1980s to around 350 channels (including dozens of foreign channels) and revenues of almost US$10 billion currently (from all sources—cable fees, pay TV, and advertising). Direct to Home (DTH) TV has become a strong catalyst for increased penetration of a growing revenue base.

India is a unique television market in Asia in that it has a very strong and very well-developed content-production infrastructure, which no other market in Asia can match. Over the past 10–12 years, India has evolved into a key growth market for satellite broadcasters, content providers, and cable networks, with some high-quality listed names. It has six DTH broadcasters, more than any other market. Zee Entertainment and its spin-off Zee News Ltd., together with soap-opera producer Balaji Telefilms Ltd., epitomize the changes that have taken place in India. These companies are led by visionary managements and have established the necessary track record and cash to continue with their growth story. The move to digitization will provide the next growth phase for Indian companies and indeed those in the rest of Asia. The Chinese market, on the other hand, has the necessary TV infrastructure and is a key Asian market for digital and high-definition TV but lacks any content-production capability, largely because of government restrictions on content.

The television landscape will look very different in India and China with the spread of digitization and the growing impetus for pay TV. According to the Hong Kong-based Cable and Satellite Broadcasting Association of Asia (CASBAA), the Asian market is growing rapidly, especially in India and China, and the pay-TV market has reached 300 million subscribers across 15 nations. Japanese cable-network operator J-COM Co. Ltd. has been one of the biggest beneficiaries of the trend toward digitization, with the bulk of its subscribers now opting for high-definition services.

The regulatory environment and piracy are key stumbling blocks in a number of markets and efforts to control these will lead to an even stronger boom in the television markets across the region. Vietnam and Malaysia provide good examples for others such as the Philippines, Thailand, and Indonesia of how governments should approach the problems of piracy.

Lifestyle companies that have begun to reflect growth in disposable incomes include breweries such as Tsingtao Breweries, which is partly owned by Anheuser-Busch. The company dominates in China's fragmented beer market and is also China's largest beer exporter, selling to 30 countries. Tsingtao has been largely instrumental in triggering the consolidation of the Chinese beer market with a spate of acquisitions. San Miguel plays a similar role in the Philippines. These are typically low-margin businesses, but these companies have only scratched the surface of their potential.

Chapter 3

Asia's Infrastructure Build-Out: The Next Great Investment Opportunity

The trends that propelled Japan, Taiwan, and South Korea into the ranks of developed nations are now unfolding with varying intensities across several Asian nations. Rapid industrialization backed by infrastructure spending, growing entrepreneurship, privatization, rapid technology absorption, developing inland trade, and a growing service sector are the core trends in China, India, Vietnam, Indonesia, Malaysia, the Philippines, Israel, and, to varying degrees, in the GCC countries.

The key to Asia's economic success that will help it fully unleash its true potential is the development of its physical, human, and financial capital and infrastructure. The physical infrastructure comprises the sum total of the roads, railways, highways, airports, water, electricity, and telecommunications that drive and enable faster and more productive economic activity.

Infrastructure: Building Pipelines and Lifelines

In China, and in several other governments of Asia, the executive power charges itself both with the reparations of the high roads, and with the maintenance of the navigable canals. The judgment formed of the governor of each province is regulated by the attention he pays to this task. This branch of public [policy] accordingly is said to be very much attended to in all those countries, but particularly in China.

—Adam Smith, *The Wealth of Nations*

While the above synopsis could well be a reflection of the importance of infrastructure in China and other Asian nations today, this account was given by the Scottish economist Adam Smith in 1776.

Travelers to China today will readily testify to the impressive scale and depth of its infrastructure and the remarkably short time span in which it has been implemented. And it is not just China that is pumping money into infrastructure; according to a Deutsche Bank report, India will be investing US$450 billion in various infrastructure sectors by 2012. Of this investment, the energy sector is likely to get the bulk of the investment (energy investments and related companies are dealt with in greater depth in Chapter 6), while roads, railways, and, more importantly, water infrastructure are expected to get US$50 billion each. The three key areas in infrastructure spending likely to drive investments are urban infrastructure, energy, and water, and physical infrastructure such as roads, ports, and highways. This was a sector of importance to governments before the slowdown; since the global meltdown infrastructure investments have taken an even greater emphasis.

While roads, highways, and ports continue to be of great importance and are the focus of fevered activity across Asia, in China it is the availability of potable water, its supply, distribution, care of its waterways, and treatment of wastewater that it is now absorbing the attention of the government. Questions over the sustainability of water resources for human consumption will become increasingly urgent as the world's population growth is expected to concentrate in Asia. According to the UN Population Fund, of the nine billion people expected to be on the planet by 2050 around 55 percent are expected to be in Asia, with nearly three billion concentrated in China and India.

While per-capita water consumption has been increasing year on year for several years, water reserves have declined by 7–10 percent a year over the past several years. This problem is compounded by the increasingly high levels of pollution in China's waterways that limits potable supply to residences and industry. According to the China Hydraulic Engineering Society, China's multi-decade boom has left its rivers and lakes severely polluted. This is all the more alarming considering that China has 8 percent of the world's fresh water reserves (which have been badly managed) and 22 percent of the world's population to supply. And it only gets worse from here; two-thirds of China's rivers are now polluted, many of them severely. Nearly 90 percent of source water for urban areas is contaminated, and 80 percent of sewage in China flows, untreated, into waterways.

To add to this very dismal picture, annual rainfall has also reduced, further affecting stocks of fresh water. Reservoir levels have dropped to their lowest levels in years, but demand for water is accelerating in the face of industrialization, urbanization, and the economic and population boom in coastal areas.

The Chinese government is responding to this potentially devastating resource crisis as only it can: with massive doses of capital investment and blanket financial and policy support to global and domestic firms engaged in various water and wastewater infrastructure programs. Not surprisingly, the urban water-supply industry has been listed as a key industry in China's 11th Five-Year Plan that runs through 2010. The government has allocated a total capital of RMB1 trillion (approximately US$150 billion) for the water sector, of which RMB300 million is for sewage and water reclamation. There is a US$51 billion allocation within China's 2008 stimulus plan for water, wastewater, and sewage treatment. Typically, water supply and wastewater management falls within the purview of the individual municipalities, which operate through majority-owned companies in which global water supply and treatment companies are now being invited to hold stakes through a bidding process.

Veolia Water, the world's largest private water-services company and a division of the French company Veolia Environment (VIE), is one of the biggest operators and builders of water projects throughout China. VIE had revenues of €36.2 billion (US$53 billion) for 2008 (13.4 percent growth over 2007) and a net income of €405 million (US$ 595 million). Veolia Water owns 49 percent in Tianjin Shibei Water Company Ltd., a company that holds a 30-year concession to supply drinking water to the city of Tianjin, one of China's fastest-growing financial centers. In addition, Veolia Water is also involved with one of China's first public–private partnerships for complete water services in Pudong, where it has a 50-year concession covering 2.65 million people to supply water and maintain all water-related services. It has two other very significant concessions in Shenzhen and Changzhou covering another six million people. The Veolia Environment stock trades at a 35 P/E on the NYSE and reflects the fact that the company has a leadership position in water services and wastewater management across the world. The valuation of the company reflects its strong positioning, focus on very high growth markets, and the strength of its balance sheet. The company has remained conservative in its financing, constantly using cash flow and asset-mix management to reduce debt and fund its significant capital requirement through internal accruals. It has a solid operating pedigree in the water business, having been granted a water concession by Emperor Napoleon III in 1853. It has been in the water business since then, and China is most likely its next growth engine. The company has also won contracts to set up and manage water infrastructure in Saudi Arabia, Dubai, and Abu Dhabi. The company's multifaceted involvement in Asia will resurface again when we come to discuss urban transportation and alternative energy systems.

The other big global names in China's water-services business are Suez Environment, Thames Water Plc (a unit of German utility RWE AG), and Berlinwasser International AG, a leading German water company that began operations in China in 1997 with a wastewater treatment facility. There are no major Chinese or, for that matter, Asian companies of the scale, technical ability, and size as these, all of which have identified China as a major growth area and have spent years (and in some cases decades) studying the market and acquiring stakes in valuable water franchises across the country. They already have much-needed domestic traction and cash flow and, since the Chinese government is not discriminating between non-Chinese and Chinese companies, they have a significant advantage in that they enjoy the confidence of local governments.

Suez Environment is another French water, waste-management, and energy giant and part of one of the world's oldest companies, with over 180 years of continuous operating history. Suez Environment has been active in China since the 1970s and currently has 23 joint ventures in 17 municipalities, with equity stakes that range from 35–50 percent (including a joint venture servicing the fast-growing region of Macau), and five joint ventures in the waste-management business. The company is considered to be one of the pioneers in the public–private partnership (PPP) approach to infrastructure development and has established its first R&D center for industrial water supply and wastewater-treatment research. In 2008 it had 65,000 employees worldwide and generated revenues of €12.5 billion (US$18.2 billion), of which China, its fastest-growing segment, produced €750 million (US$1.1 billion). Like Veolia Environment, the company has targeted significant growth from all of Asia. In mid-2009, it won a major contract in Abu Dhabi with a 15-year concession to manage a €200 million (US$290 million) hazardous-waste project. As discussed earlier, Abu Dhabi too is emerging as another major market for water and wastewater-management infrastructure. The position of French companies is helped in no small measure by the involvement of the French government in putting collaborative frameworks in place with governments in Asia. A case in point is the cooperation agreement on water resources signed between the French and Chinese governments, which essentially enhances French involvement in water management, infrastructure building, and supply in China.

Israel has developed considerable expertise in water management and treatment (in desalination, purification, and reclamation, in particular) over several decades. The country, which is two-thirds arid, has one of the best water-management systems in the world. Its municipal water-loss rate (9.7 percent) is less than half that of the European average and it reclaims an unparalleled 75 percent of the water it uses. The Israeli government and companies (300 of which are involved in the wastewater-treatment industry alone) have been very forthcoming in offering their expertise in China and elsewhere in Asia. Amiad Filtration Systems Ltd., a global supplier of filters and filtration systems, is one Israeli company that stands out since it provided the sewage and wastewater-treatment services during the Beijing Olympics in 2008. Though small (its revenues for 2008 totaled US$75 million), the company is very profitable, with an operating margin of 46 percent and one-year revenue growth of 29 percent. It has for the most part focused on US and Central Europe and has only begun to tap the potential in Asia, which is widely expected to drive its revenue growth and profitability. It has recently become involved with projects in India, Singapore, and Malaysia in the steel and petrochemical industries, and has won a number of tenders for projects in Chile and Brazil in the agricultural, oil and gas, and mining sectors.

The Singapore government too has taken a very focused and active interest in working with the Chinese government in finding policy and technology solutions to its water crisis. Several high-tech companies in water treatment operate out of Singapore. Ultra-Flo Pte. Ltd. (a privately held company), for example, uses proprietary technology in the manufacture of hollow fiber ultra-filtration membranes used in integrated water and wastewater treatment. Dayen International provides integrated systems for waste and water-treatment systems for large-scale engineering projects. The Singapore Ministry of Trade and Industry has partnered with the Asian Development Bank (ADB) to create a platform to provide technology and share knowledge with companies building water infrastructure in China. The ADB and three privately held Singapore companies—United Engineers Singapore, The Konzen Group, and Crest Spring Private Ltd.—have formed a consortium called the Asia Infrastructure Project Development Private Ltd. that seeks to provide technical and management skills for ADB-funded water projects across Asia, though the primary focus is public–private partnership ventures with local governments and municipalities in China.

Hyflux Ltd. has made significant inroads into the Chinese wastewater-treatment and water-recycling market, with an operating presence in 35 individual projects in 26 provinces; a relationship that has been built over the last 20 years. It is also setting up used-oil recycling centers in Beijing and a couple of other cities. The company has very strong financial and operating metrics and has reported a compounded revenue growth of 46 percent and a 22 percent growth in EPS over the last five years. Its operating margins and return on equity are among the highest for the sector, and the stock typically trades at a premium. However, the fact that the balance sheet is highly geared relative to its peers is probably not the best characteristic considering the current global economic environment. Sembcorp and Darco Water Technologies Ltd. are other Singapore technology companies establishing a presence in China's wastewater-treatment industry.

The Chinese government is acutely aware of the need to encourage private and foreign participation in developing and managing its water infrastructure. It has also taken a very pragmatic approach toward the pricing of water services, with a tiered pricing structure depending on usage. China's Ministry of Water Resources has said that it will use price as a lever to influence water conservation. Wastewater treatment, for example, cost the equivalent of US1¢ per ton in 2005 and is expected to cost consumers 10¢ per ton in 2010–11. The tiered pricing concept is applied to all categories of consumers, whether industrial, residential, or agricultural. Thus the operating environment makes the wastewater-treatment industry a very lucrative one. Overall, the Chinese water-infrastructure industry is very conducive to business, where companies enjoy long-term concessions, supportive government policies, an attractive pricing environment, and a growing population base.

With one of the world's longest coastlines, China is also the largest emerging market for desalination facilities. According to some estimates, the Chinese market for water treatment is worth around US$80 billion, of which desalination already accounts for almost 10 percent. Desalination as a water-supply alternative is expected to grow significantly over the next few years, and the volume of water produced is expected to accelerate from its current level of 40 million gallons per day to close to 264 million gallons per day by 2010–11. Very few of the consumables and equipment required to run desalination plants, such as high-pressure pumps and energy-recovery devices, are actually manufactured in China and the industry is therefore dependent on foreign firms and foreign technology to accelerate desalination investments.

Singapore's Hyflux Ltd., for example, is building one of the largest desalination plants (with a capacity to produce 40 million gallons per day) for US$155 million.

Across most Chinese cities and towns the piping system is more than 50 years old and, according to Chinese government estimates, 37 percent of pipes need to be replaced. In addition to replacement demand, the increased activity in water supply and wastewater treatment is leading to a massive double-digit growth in demand for all types of pipes, particularly large-diameter pipes. Pre-stressed concrete cylinder pipes are the major material used in the supply of potable water. In addition to this is the demand for pipes for supplying gas and chemicals for industry. High-density polyethylene pipes are used in gas transmission, while reinforced thermoset plastic is used for transporting chemicals to China's process industries. This combined demand has created the single largest market in the world for large-diameter pipes, for which the pipe industry anticipates rapid growth.

Urban renewal and growth are key drivers for companies in this business and the larger and more densely populated the cities, the greater the need for sanitation and water pipes. China has 171 cities with more than a million people while India has 56, making these two countries major players in this form of infrastructure. Companies such as Insituform Technologies Inc., which makes pressure pipes and offers complete solutions, could benefit from all this demand growth. The company has been growing in India, Hong Kong, and Australia and now has set its sights on Singapore and China.

Another regional company to watch out for is Jeddah-based Saudi Arabian Amiantit Company, a 40-year-old leading manufacturer of pipes and accessories for fluid systems. Seeing the opportunity unfold as domestic and regional investments in water supply and treatment systems accelerate, through a Germany-based subsidiary, Aquamundo GmbH, Amiantit diversified into building, operating, and managing water supply globally, with an emphasis on emerging Europe and China. The Saudi company owns 30 pipe-manufacturing plants across 19 countries, six technology companies, and a number of engineering subsidiaries around the globe, including a new R&D unit (employing 100 engineers) in Pune, India. The company reported revenues of US$1.2 billion for 2008. However, the company has nearly 50 percent of its two-year average revenues as receivables, and this trend of rising receivables needs to be investigated adequately before taking any investment action. The company also has very close links with the Saudi royal family, at least two of whom are government ministers and sit on the board of directors.

The massive investment in water infrastructure and wastewater management in China has had an effect too on the manufacture of valves and centrifugal pumps, where the global average growth has generally been in low single digits every year. However, driven by its municipal spending on water, sewage, and water treatment, the Chinese segment has been growing by 15 percent annually. The US-based Flowserve Corporation, a leader in valves, pumps, and seals in the oil and chemicals industry, is spreading its expertise to the water sector in Asia. It already has a manufacturing presence in China, India, and Saudi Arabia, among other places.

In essence, companies related to all aspects of the supply and treatment of water and related waste-disposal infrastructure have a fertile environment in China and in most of Asia as water has now gone to the top of the infrastructure policy agenda in several countries.

The GCC nations in the Middle East have plans to invest roughly US$120 billion in water supply, recycling, and wastewater-treatment plants over the next few years, and this will provide another opportunity for many of the global and Asian players currently displaying their skills in China. A company that is well positioned to benefit from this regional investment surge is Dubai-based Metito Overseas, which has more than 50 years of operating experience in the area of water supply, wastewater treatment, and desalination. In recent years the company has concentrated its operations in the Middle East, Southeast Asia, India, and, to some extent, in North Africa. In a recent joint venture with Berlinwasser International AG it has already bid for US$1 billion-worth of projects in the GCC countries and expects to be the dominant player as further lucrative contracts in water supply, treatment, and desalination systems are rolled out in the near future. Metito Overseas is currently a private company, but discussions are under way for the probable launch of an IPO in 2010, which will offer investors a chance to partake of a huge growth sector in the Middle East.

Malaysia's Salcon Berhad is a small water and environment engineering specialist operating in three Chinese provinces. Despite its small size (2008 revenues of US$70 million), Salcon has completed projects in

Malaysia, Indonesia, Vietnam, Thailand, and India and has secured five water-supply contracts in China. The Malaysian water market is currently subject to new legislation designed to better regulate the industry and eventually lead to further growth in the sector. Salcon intends to focus on the domestic market, where US$3 billion-worth of projects are being implemented. The impact of winning new contracts will be strongly felt given the smaller revenue base, as evidenced by a 76 percent increase in revenues during the first quarter of 2009. The balance sheet too is con-servatively financed, with a debt-to-capital ratio of 0.3 percent.

Japanese water-treatment specialist Kurita Water Industries Ltd. produces chemicals and equipment and, like other Japanese companies in the water industry, has built up technologies in water systems and products. Other leading Japanese companies are Kubota Corp., JFE Holdings Inc., Sumitomo Heavy Industries, and Maruichi Steel Tubes.

Given its rapid industrial growth and continuing urbanization, South Korea is vulnerable to potential water and food shortages. Korean com-panies have built size and expertise, especially in water management and infrastructure: companies such as Daewoo Engineering & Construction, Hyundai Engineering & Construction, Doosan Heavy Industry, and Korea Express, though widely diversified across the infrastructure spec-trum, are also leaders in the water industry.

Water remains a key infrastructure need in India too. Ensuring water supply and wastewater treatment for a complex and growing web of urban centers is becoming increasingly important. IVRCL Infrastructure Ltd., an infrastructure-development company, has built expertise in water projects across the country. Companies such as Electrosteel Casting, which manu-factures ductile iron pipes (which are superior to traditional concrete pipes and growing in demand), and Thermax Ltd., a market leader in water-purification technology and products, are key players here.

A good way to gain exposure to the feverish pace of growth in so many Asian economies is to invest in infrastructure funds such as the Sarasin Sustainable Water Fund, which is managed by the Swiss private bank, Bank Sarasin, which in turn is owned by Rabobank of the Netherlands. Another way is through the Claymore S&P Global Water Index ETF, which tracks the S&P Global Water Index, which in turn represents the top 50 global water stocks (both utilities and equipment suppliers). While only around 10 percent of the companies represent Asia, many have varying degrees of exposure to Asia (Veolia Environment and Suez Environment are both amply represented). Also of note is the PowerShares Water Resources Portfolio ETF.

Asia's Infrastructure Requirement: Diverse Needs of a Diverse Continent

Given their rapid industrial growth over the past several years, a number of key Asian economies have had a great need for massive infrastructure spending. Implementing infrastructure projects in most cases, however, has been tardy. The expectation of large infrastructure investments outside of China has not been satisfactorily met. While the world has been mesmerized by Chinese physical infrastructure investments in recent years, it has forgotten that the Southeast Asian nations that led economic growth in the 1990s have made few significant additions to their infrastructure over the past decade. Capital investments stopped almost entirely in the aftermath of the 1997–98 Asian crisis, when capital formation as a percentage of GDP dropped from 40 percent to 20 percent. In Thailand, this has recovered to around 27 percent in recent years, but in Malaysia and the Philippines it has remained stagnant at below 20 percent.

Fortunately, policy makers have realized that this state of neglect has to change and have put measures in place to develop their domestic markets. Indonesia and Malaysia, for example, have given clear demonstrations that there is a political will to deal with the problems. In the Philippines too, where little had been done to address the country's pressing infrastructure needs, the government now plans to spend 4 percent of its GDP on infrastructure development. The Philippine Investment Priority Plan proposes a greater role for foreign investors in the US$15 billion infrastructure plan for the period up to 2011.

Asia needs very significant investments in roads, railways, airports, sanitation, conventional and alternative energy, and all kinds of urban and rural infrastructure. The limitations of poor infrastructure in many Asian nations and the consequent impact of lost or diminished productivity is now very well understood, and, in the face of the global slowdown, national governments have made infrastructure spending their number-one priority. Given the importance now being placed on the domestic economy, the focus is very likely to be on the development of road and rail networks and logistics infrastructure such as container terminal facilities.

As we saw earlier, China is already the world's largest manufacturer of cars, and India's new small car, the Nano, will accelerate automotive growth in India very significantly. In fact, in light of the response to the Nano's launch in the summer of 2009 Tata Motors expects to produce half a million of this model. Such numbers are forcing governments into action since less than half of the roads in any of these large Asian economies is actually paved. To fund such projects, an Asian Investment Bank, capitalized by various sovereign wealth funds from Asia and the huge pools of savings across the continent, has been proposed to seed infrastructure investment on a public–private partnership basis.

China, India, and the leading ASEAN nations have announced additional infrastructure spending between 2009–11 amounting to US$1.6 trillion, with China accounting for roughly a third of the total. India, Indonesia, Taiwan, and South Korea are expected to be serious spenders from now on, though on different aspects of their infrastructure, with the biggest change likely to be seen in Indonesia, which historically has been extremely slow to deal with its chronic infrastructure shortage. However, given the momentum of its economic growth the greatest lag in infrastructure investment is in India. The Asian Development Bank has said that Asian nations need to invest around US$8 trillion in infrastructure between 2010 and 2020 and around US$290 billion in various cross-border projects.

Though the bulk of the infrastructure thrust comes from China, some of the best Asian-domiciled investment names come from India, where private and public-sector companies have the expertise, track record, and experience necessary to implement infrastructure projects. The Mumbai-based Hindustan Construction Company is one company that has very successfully made the transformation from a construction company to an infrastructure company, having already implemented some very complex and prestigious projects. Table 3.1 shows a cross-section of publicly traded Asian infrastructure and construction companies.

Cement manufacturers and building aggregates should be key beneficiaries. Swiss cement and aggregates giant Holcim is very well entrenched in Asia, particularly in India and Indonesia (listed on the

Table 3.1: Publicly traded Asian infrastructure and construction companies

Company	Country of Domicile	Product	2008 Revenue (US$)	Revenue (5-Year CAGR)	Net Income (5-Year CAGR)	RoE 5-Year Average
Larsen & Toubro Ltd.	India	Manufacturer of heavy engineering equipment; engineering project company	$8,800 million	23%	29%	32%
IVRCL Infrastructure	India	Engineering & Construction including marine	$1,087 million	38%	32%	15%
BEML	India	Manufacturer of earth-moving equipment, excavators, wheel loaders, & other heavy machinery	$612 million	10%	8.9%	31%
BHEL	India	Manufacturer of powerplant equipment	$5,802 million	22%	27%	40%
Patel Engineering	India	Engineering & Construction	$540 million	26%	45%	29%
Hindustan Construction	India	Engineering & Construction projects in India and emerging Asia	$780 million	18%	NA	13%
Shanghai Construction	China	Building construction & infrastructure facilities	$4,274 million	17%	8%	7%

(Continued)

Table 3.1 (*Continued*)

Company	Country of Domicile	Product	2008 Revenue (US$)	Revenue (5-Year CAGR)	Net Income (5-Year CAGR)	RoE 5-Year Average
Lonking Holdings Ltd.	China	Manufacturer of wheel loaders and infrastructure equipment	$885 million	24%	38%	30%
Guangxi Liugong Machinery	China	Manufacturer of loaders, road rollers, & excavators	$1,330 million	21%	7%	18%
Doosan Heavy Industries & Construction	Korea	Manufacturer & installer of steam and hydraulic turbines, condensers, and heat exchangers	$5,289 million	18%	NA	7%
Sanby Heavy Industries	China	Manufacturer of concrete pumps, concrete pump vehicles, pavers, & road rollers	$1,975 million	34%	25%	23%
Sembcorp Industries	Singapore	Infrastructure services, including engineering and environmental, to various industries	$7,024 million	11%	5%	23%

SOURCE: Bloomberg

Jakarta Stock Exchange as PT Holcim Indonesia), where it has a strong manufacturing and distribution presence. Other strong companies are Indonesian cement giant PT Indocement; and Taiwanese cement giant Asia Cement, which has evolved into a regional player with a growing footprint in China. Grasim Industries Ltd. is one of India's best-run cement companies and controls 55 percent in Ultratech Cement, the country's largest cement company.

Transportation Infrastructure

While the development of inland trade is driving railway construction in Asia, urbanization is driving frantic investment in transport infrastructure within cities. Developing subway systems is the next big theme in India, which has some of the world's fastest-growing urban areas. Canadian company Bombardier Inc. is the big beneficiary of the expansion of the New Delhi metro, in 2008 winning an order for hundreds of new subway cars worth several hundred million dollars. Now Mumbai is looking at the phased introduction of a world-class subway system from 2010, when it will have one line operational until 2021, by which time a total of nine lines covering 146 km will be operational. Veolia Transport, a division of Veolia Environment, which holds 5 percent of the concession, will be responsible for the operation and maintenance of the entire Mumbai Metro in a joint venture with Reliance Infrastructure, which holds 69 percent. The potential in a city of Mumbai's population (20 million) and density (27,000 people per square km) is very significant, especially considering that when fully operational the metro will reduce commuting times by 70 percent and thus have a direct impact on productivity. Veolia Transport has also entered China's urban transport market for the first time through a joint venture with Nanjing Zhongbei, a company listed on the Shenzhen Stock Exchange since 1996, to operate the transportation systems (2,000 buses) in six Chinese cities for a period of 30 years. With 47 percent of Chinese expected to live in cities by 2011 the scope for mass intra-city transportation is huge. But transportation infrastructure is more than just developing rail corridors or better urban mass-transit systems; it is the entire development and management of the transport system, including the actual building out of infrastructure.

Companies such as Zhejiang Expressway Co. Ltd. and Jiangsu Expressway Co. Ltd. do exactly that. Jiangsu Expressway in particular operates a number of lucrative toll roads and provides services such as fuel stops and food outlets as well as offering construction and management of road infrastructure. Shenzhen Expressway and Sichuan Expressway are two more names experiencing growth in traffic and straddle the busiest roadways in China. Competitive pressures are bound to emerge from competing railroads that are emerging across the province but that is over the long term; meanwhile, these companies will continue their extremely profitable operations and strong cash generation.

For some time now Asia has been, and will remain, the pre-eminent global trading hub in manufactured goods. Nearly two-thirds of the world's throughput of 20-foot containers originate in Asian ports, and two-thirds of the world's top 25 container ports are Asian. Not surprising, perhaps, as these economies were export oriented the entire development focus was on port cities and surrounding areas. Now the focus has shifted to the rapid and sustainable development of the domestic economy and the hinterland, which means that there will be an added emphasis to developing a dense railway network. In addition there is likely to be a boom in domestic containerization, privatization of railway assets, and an overall increase in domestic trade infrastructure, including the setting up, expansion, or upgrading of existing road networks. China, in particular, has identified the expansion of the railway network as a key development initiative.

Some Singapore exchange listings provide some exposure to the container trade through trusts such as First Ship Lease Trusts (FSLT), Pacific Shipping Trust (PST), and Rickmers Maritime (RMT). Container shipping rates are the key driver here. Container stocks are a proxy on world trade and Asian stocks will reflect the phenomenal potential for trade growth between Asian nations. Even ship-building remains a profitable activity given the fact that the Chinese and Korean governments are not likely to allow their formidable ship-building industries to remain idle through the decline in global trade. Government-backed orders are pouring into Northeast Asian shipyards. STX Group of Korea remains an interesting play on several global trends. It is a holding company with various subsidiaries, including STX Offshore and Shipbuilding, which is the world's fourth-largest shipbuilder and owner of STX Europe, Europe's largest ship-building group. It owns shipyards in Turkey and Norway. The Turkish shipyard recently built the world's largest cruise liner for an American company. A number of its subsidiaries are seeking independent listings in Korea, Europe, and China, which will essentially strengthen the financial position of the holding company.

Domestic Trade Infrastructure

With the development of national economies now central in government thinking across the continent, investment in railways has become a priority. China is ahead of most of Asia in this category. In the RMB4 trillion (US$586 billion) Chinese stimulus plan that is scheduled to run through 2010, the highest allocation of RMB1.5 trillion (US$220 billion) is for transportation infrastructure, of which the bulk has been allocated to railways. This indicates that the Chinese are gearing up for an upswing in domestic trade and for a boost to the power infrastructure (boosting coal transportation has been specifically mentioned as a stimulus objective).

In countries like India and China where domestic trade is carried out across vast distances, the growth, modernization, and expansion of railway networks and airports will have to become a priority. Companies such as India-based Jindal Steel & Power Ltd., the country's largest manufacturer of rails, and Chinese railway companies, including rolling-stock manufacturers, will be major beneficiaries. The completion of the world's highest railway—the Qinghai–Tibet line—underscored China's rail development plans and brought the company that built it, China Railway Construction Corp. (CRCC), to public attention. Its listing in 2008 was one of the most wildly popular IPOs to come out of China. CRCC's revenues compounded by 21 percent and its operating income by 35 percent over the five-year period to 2008 and the company's order book indicates that the top-line growth momentum is likely to continue at around 20 percent for the next few years. The company continues to make significant annual investments in its fixed capital base (around 20 percent growth in assets annually), which is a key driver.

Logistics and freight company Container Corporation of India is the largest inland container handler in India, with a 90 percent market share of the container traffic. It hauls containers from ports to inland destinations on its owned railway wagons. The key to Container Corp.'s continued success is the fact that it is difficult for competitors to establish themselves given its relationship with the Indian railways (which are entirely state-owned), and the fact that its cost base will be extremely hard to replicate. Among China's logistics companies, Shenzhen International Holdings Ltd. builds and operates logistics infrastructure facilities, including toll roads and logistics parks in China. It is 40 percent owned by the Shenzhen municipal government.

Daquin Railway Company is a freight operator hauling coal across China. Given the importance being placed on coal-fired power plants and metal production the company is likely to witness growth, and in recent months has made several acquisitions. The Chinese railway network is split into different regions and, given the operational complexities and cost-and-efficiency needs, these are very likely to be consolidated and given to companies such as Daquin Railway to operate. This will ensure the company's earnings growth, as many of the segments likely to be amalgamated are lucrative routes linked with key cities or coal-producing regions.

Agricultural Infrastructure: From Farm Gate to Supermarket Shelf

Both India and China have benefited significantly from agricultural reforms that raised agricultural output and eliminated the need to import basic food grains in the 1970s. But while this "Green Revolution" lifted India and China into self-sufficiency in food, it also greatly increased their reliance on genetically modified seeds and chemical fertilizers.

Despite the successes, however, 40 percent of farm produce in India is destroyed or spoils even before it leaves the farms. According to a study by Ernst & Young and the Federation of Indian Chambers of Commerce and Industry (FICCI), India is one of the largest producers of fruits, vegetables, milk, and meat products in the world but has the lowest yield among major producing nations. The creation of cold chains—a series of refrigerated warehouses in major agricultural centers, with a focus on ventilation, sanitation, and temperature control—and refrigerated transport facilities will increase the longevity of fresh produce and meat, and the chemicals and enzymes used in the pharmaceutical and chemical industries. This effort will also boost investment and create massive employment in the food-processing industry. In India, the food-processing, retail, pharmaceutical, and logistics companies are now integrating their efforts to produce a national cold-chain infrastructure, and the cold-chain industry is growing at 20–25 percent per annum. By 2015, it is expected to be a US$10 billion industry. Smaller listed Indian logistics companies such as Allcargo Global Logistics (2009 revenues of US$540 million) are well positioned to break into this very lucrative growth market. The company already has a network of warehouses connected to container freight stations linked to both ports and inland destinations.

As Asia grows richer there is a greater demand for animal proteins and for animal-feed producers. New Hope Agribusiness Co. Ltd. (NHA), based in Sichuan province, is the largest animal-feed producer in China, with close to US$1 billion in annual revenues. Listed on the Shenzhen Exchange since 1998, the company is the only listed subsidiary of the New Hope Group, one of China's largest privately owned enterprises (with annual revenues of US$7 billion). The Hope Group's strong management has delivered very rapid and profitable growth and has shown leadership to the feed industry during a very difficult time. The feed industry in China has suffered in recent months from several contamination scandals that have largely hit the smaller producers who have not upgraded their quality-control facilities. According to China's Agriculture Ministry, the feed market is highly fragmented, with 15,000 companies producing a total of 131 million tons per annum, of which NHA controls 7 percent. The government has closed down the operations of hundreds of feed producers that have inadequate quality control or whose feed was contaminated with melamine, and has begun to destroy thousands of tons of contaminated feed, thus driving up feed prices. The company has experienced lower profit margins in recent years largely as a result of the rising cost of soya bean meal and corn, which are major raw materials, but the combination of higher feed prices and reduced competition is working in New Hope's favor. Higher feed prices are unlikely to upset demand from pig farmers, who now receive government subsidies to offset the higher prices as part of its economic stimulus package. A key driver for the company is therefore the live pig population, which is expected to rise to it highest level ever over the next few years. The company also has a leadership position in the less-fragmented pig-feed markets in Southeast Asia, especially Vietnam and the Philippines, where it enjoys stronger margins than it does in China.

The company has also expanded into dairy products hoping to extend its brand and reputation for quality into other food segments. Its growth here is very likely to include acquisitions of other Chinese dairy producers such as the recent acquisition of a dairy firm in Inner Mongolia. This strategy, though, will bring it into direct competition with the Hong Kong-listed Mengniu Dairy, China's largest dairy firm, and the Shanghai-listed Inner Mongolia Yili Industrial Group. Both of these companies have revenues of roughly US$3.5 billion and both have been hurt in the tainted-milk scandal that hit China in 2008. First-quarter figures for 2009, however, show an improvement in both revenues and net income. In comparison, New Hope Agribusiness reports under US$150 million annually from the dairy business, but this is expected to grow rapidly.

One of the largest and possibly oldest players in Asia's agri-industrial and food-processing industries is the Stock Exchange of Thailand-listed Charoen Pokhpand Foods Ltd. The company has a 90-year operating history and has been under the same family management throughout. The company is very well established in Thailand with several complementary business lines in animal and aquatic feeds, livestock breeding, meat and fish production, and food processing. The company has a reputation for being quality conscious and its processed-foods products are sold within East Asia and the European Union. Another market-dominating play from Thailand is Thai President Foods Ltd., which holds a 50 percent market share of Thailand's instant and flavored noodle market.

China is expected to be one of the fastest-growing food-processing markets in the world. Significant opportunities exist for global food processors and marketing organizations. Danone has developed significant Chinese and Southeast Asian operations. China and Indonesia are now its two largest markets for baby formula. Growth rates in these markets are roughly 20 percent annually. Another global company seeing significant growth in the Chinese baby-formula market is Mead Johnson Nutrition. But Tokyo-based Yakult Honsha Co. Ltd. may benefit more than most. It is already seeing its profits expand as a result of its Chinese and Southeast Asian operations and this is expected to gain momentum over the next two or three years. Global consulting firm McKinsey & Company expects the Chinese urban food market to become a US$1 trillion market by 2025.

Given world agriculture's focus on crop yields, the use of chemical fertilizers is only likely to rise, despite all the well-documented environmental drawbacks. While fertilizer manufacturers crisscross Asia, some of the most competitive fertilizer stocks are to be found in the Middle East. Saudi Arabian Fertilizer Company (SAFCO), SABIC, and Kuwait Chemicals are located closest to the natural gas that is the core raw material for fertilizer production. These companies and others such as Jordanian company Arab Potash all enjoy very significant returns on equity. SAFCO, in particular, has grown very quickly and compounded revenues at nearly 20 percent annually for the last 10 years. China-based Qinghai Salt Lake Potash is another strong growth candidate, producing potassic fertilizers, and is a very profitable company.

Israel's Micro-Irrigation Know-How

Like much of the world, Asia is turning to Israel for micro-irrigation (drip irrigation) technology. Israeli companies hold 50 percent of the global drip-irrigation market. The world's largest provider of drip-irrigation technology and products is Netafim Ltd., which has a 45-year operating history. The company, which pioneered the technology, has operations in 110 countries and revenues in excess of US$500 million. The company has been focusing on Asia and on India, in particular, where it has two manufacturing plants.

The Middle East as an Emerging Infrastructure Destination

The Middle East region is among the world's newest industrializing economies, with a very fast-growing and sophisticated domestic service economy in areas such as insurance, banking, asset management, telecom, infrastructure, healthcare, and hospitality. A number of these companies are also the direct result of privatization by the government. The changing face of the Middle East is a key facet of the change unfolding in Asia. The oil-rich countries have seen a number of past commodity cycles that flooded them with cash, most of which was squandered. But with the substantial increases in oil prices witnessed in the mid-2000s, for the first time these nations, some of them little more than city-states, have attempted to seriously move away from oil dependence and diversify into the industrial and service sectors.

A key element of this transformation is in transportation infrastructure and the rich emirate of Qatar is now at the center of the region's rush to create this infrastructure. Qatar, which has the world's largest reserves of natural gas, has a total population of less than one million people and is the world's richest nation on a per-capita basis. In partnership with Deutsche Bahn AG, the German national railway infrastructure company, it is investing US$25 billion in railway infrastructure that will include a high-speed rail link connecting the capital city, Doha, with the airport. It will also build freight corridors between Qatari cities and its other Persian Gulf neighbors, and a metro system in the capital city. The Saudis are spending $5 billion to build inter-city, high-speed rail links. The city of Dubai has already opened the Persian Gulf's first subway system and its sister city, Abu Dhabi, is now doing feasibility studies into creating its own subway system. The Yemen Arab Republic, too, is looking to build freight corridors to its more prosperous neighbors such as Saudi Arabia, while Iraq seeks to invest heavily in rebuilding its seaports.

The Qatari venture will attract other European and Asian railway companies into the Middle East to take advantage of government plans to spend around US$100 billion on transport infrastructure alone. This could also spur the likely privatization of Deutsche Bahn AG or of some of its subsidiaries as it seeks to raise the capital it needs to invest its share of the project outlay. A privatization of some part of DB AG is currently being considered by the German government.

The efforts of the oil-rich emirates and sheikdoms to industrialize and transform themselves into post-industrial societies will benefit domestic investors and global corporations alike. Local companies such as Saudi Telecom (the Arab world's largest telecom company with a US$25 billion market capitalization and exposure to emerging markets from India, Indonesia, and Malaysia), Mobile Telecommunications Co. Ltd. of Kuwait (US$15 billion in market capitalization and US$7.5 billion in revenues), and Dubai Ports World Ltd. (US$7.2 billion market capitalization) are good ways to gain exposure to this region (despite Dubai Ports World Ltd.'s parent company's debt problems) since they are quasi-monopolies with strong government backing and near-impenetrable competitive advantages.

Chapter 4

Building Brands but Keeping an Eye on Traditional Strengths

For the most part, the world has focused on Asia's manufacturing prowess, its ability to produce low-cost, low-value-added goods, and its ability to outsource IT-related services to remote back offices. The reality is that Asia has become home to some very powerful domestic brands that have either been supported by closed economies or by breakthroughs in the export market. As these markets develop, emerging and, in several cases, well-established brands have now become a very significant investment theme in countries like China, India, Taiwan, Indonesia, Vietnam, and South Korea.

It is this building of local brands across Asia that underscores the emergence of a powerful domestic economy. Globally, brands from emerging Asia are generally recognizable only in the consumer electronics, computer, and white-goods industries. Apart from the well-recognized Korean brands, most of these are Taiwanese and concentrated in the consumer-electronics sector, such as Acer, ASUS, D-Link, HTC, and TrendMicro. In most other sectors, Asian brands are either not quite visible or not yet considered trustworthy. But in the domestic markets it is a very different story. There are a number of brands emerging in a wide variety of industries, especially in China and India. *BusinessWeek* magazine recently referred to China as an emerging brand powerhouse with powerful brands such as Lenovo (its most recognizable brand overseas), Huawei, and China Mobile. Asian consumers have become extremely brand conscious and are not averse to spending on premium products if the brand appeals to them.

India too has a fair share of domestic brands and many have a long history. For example, the cola brand Thums Up was introduced into India in the late 1970s after Coca-Cola was asked to shut down its bottling operations during the peak of India's industry nationalization program. It grew into a very powerful brand and, in the early 1990s, Coca-Cola bought it and continued to invest in the brand. Thums Up now forms a significant portion of Coca-Cola's sales in India and gives it an edge over its rival Pepsi. The cola is even exported to countries with sizeable Indian expatriate populations.

Certain Indian bottled-water brands or Chinese spirits brands are strong but localized players in their respective countries and little known outside. Yantai Changyu Pioneer Wine Company, for example, produces a wide range of spirits and has inherited the brands and the legacy of a wine and brandy distiller that was founded well over a century ago. While Changyu has not made a major splash outside of China, Tsingtao, a major domestic Chinese beer brand is sold globally. While Hong Kong-listed appliance maker Gome Electrical Appliances Holdings Ltd. has struggled financially in recent quarters and has never shaken off its reputation for poor corporate governance, it essentially remains a bet on China's consuming class and its own brand prowess. The company has a 10 percent share of the Chinese appliances market.

One common element among these brands is the fact that they were created and grown during an era of protectionism, but they also offered very good value to consumers, which is why they have endured and represent remarkable investment potential.

Several home-grown Indian and Chinese auto manufacturers epitomize the new aggressive mindset, following in the footsteps of their more illustrious counterparts in Japan and Korea in using their well-established, large, and profitable domestic presence to access world markets. The domination of the global auto industry by Japanese brands is well known. Even though US and European car makers have purchased or have alliances with several Japanese brands, the top manufacturers remain purely Japanese. The Korean auto makers Hyundai, in the 1990s, and, more recently, KIA Motors began to produce globally competitive models and dominated niche areas. Now the emerging auto-players from China and India are adding to the mix.

The acquisition of global brands seems to be the preferred step for emerging Asian auto companies to gain market share, technology, and, more importantly, name recognition. Tata Motors' acquisition of iconic British brands Jaguar and Range Rover signals the arrival of one more Asian automotive company with major global ambitions. Chinese auto companies have so far been unlucky in their choice of targets or partners in their quest to acquire a major global brand. The attempted purchase of GM's Hummer brand by the government-run Sichuan Tengzhong Heavy Industrial Machinery Co. is an example of the hunt for trophy brands which would mark the arrival of Chinese manufacturing brands, even though in this case it would not be a value-accretive acquisition. The proposed purchase also puts the company at odds with Chinese state policy that promotes fuel efficiency and green technologies more than anything else. The efforts of Beijing Automotive Industries Holding Co. (BAIC) to buy GM's Swedish brand SAAB failed when its acquisition partner, Swedish sportscar maker Koeningsegg Group AB, backed out of the deal. BAIC also failed in its bid to buy Opel, another GM brand, and SAIC Motors had to write down its investment in Korea's Ssangyong Motors.

At the time of writing, Geely Automobile Holdings, in partnership with a Chinese government-backed investor, announced its interest in buying Volvo from Ford Motors. Eventually, Chinese companies will succeed in making major brand acquisitions overseas; meanwhile, Chinese auto brands are roaring in the domestic market. At the 2009 Shanghai Auto Expo, Geely unveiled 22 different models, including premium models, signaling confidence in its ability to compete with all the major global brands in China.

Outside of automobiles, Haier Electronics Group Co. Ltd. is a growing success story both within and outside China in the electronic-appliances space. It is fairly well recognized overseas, and, following a number of small acquisitions, is now the third-largest appliance brand in the US.

A number of leading and fast-growing Chinese brands are the result of the efforts of new, first-generation entrepreneurs or derive from the privatization or public listing of once-stodgy state-owned enterprises. The financial sector provides good examples of the latter: ICBC, Bank of Communications, Ping An, and China Life Insurance (which we will discuss in greater detail in Chapter 5). In today's China there is ample room for entrepreneurs to start up and to grow, as we have seen with the founders of Baidu.com, commonly known as China's Google; Alibaba.com; the property developer Vanke; BYD Co., the country's number-one maker of electric cars and recharge-able batteries; and the lesser-known but equally entrepreneurial Vision China, which creates and sells advertising in Beijing's public-transit system. Incidentally, the founder of BYD Co., Wang Chuanfu, was a fresh addition to the Forbes billionaire list in 2009.

The emergence of Asian brands is a key stage in the evolution of Asian business and marks the development of unique identities that in some cases have become local icons and in other cases have become very strong global brands. In each of these cases these brands have now become capable of delivering value. While India has seen the emergence of its local brands over several decades of protectionism, Chinese brands are just evolving and are moving in sync with increasing entrepreneurship. With a growing proportion of the Chinese economy in private hands, the focus on brand creation and brand-driven values is now critical and will become more so. According to China's National Bureau of Statistics the number of privately owned enterprises grew by 81 percent between 2004 and 2008 to reach 3.6 million, while the number of state-owned enterprises (SOE) dropped by 20 percent to 143,000. In this same period the private enterprises' share of total assets by value rose by 3.3 percentage points to 12.3 percent.

Global advertising and marketing companies have not missed the opportunity and are attempting to grow with Asian brands in these markets. WPP Group Plc, the world's largest advertising, marketing, and communications company (with brands such as Ogilvy & Mather, JWT, and Hill and Knowlton), has begun to make major inroads into Asia and has also been growing through acquisitions. WPP is well positioned as multinationals begin to make their presence felt in China. However, though fast-growing, the Chinese advertising market is fragmented and subject to cut-throat pricing and thus not very profitable. Currently, 16 percent of WPP's market-research business is generated from emerging Asia, while its advertising revenue share is likely less than one-sixth of its total revenues, although these are also likely to grow at a faster pace over the next few years.

Demand for quality products has revolutionized manufacturing and is driving brand awareness. It is in the domestic arena that brands are emerging and will be a great source of value. As domestic demand takes off with highly localized tastes it also drives the growth and value of Asian brands. However, true Asian brands—for the most part clustered in the consumer-electronics, IT hardware, and mobile-phone handset industries—do not yet have a strong presence in the global arena and their potential value is very low at the moment. An Interbrand survey in 2008 showed that just 6 percent of respondents in developed markets would be willing to buy a brand made in China (as opposed to a wider acceptance for popular global brands that may be outsourced from China).

The central thesis in this book is that the real desire and opportunity is for greater economic integration within Asia. As a consequence, the opportunity for local brands to grow throughout the region as a prelude to going global is very tangible.

Asian competitiveness is now spread across several sectors: software development and IT services in India; flat-panel televisions in Taiwan; consumer electronics in China and Japan; electronic components in Malaysia; shipbuilding and electronics (especially computer monitors) in South Korea; coal and iron-ore mining in Indonesia; and polymers and fertilizers in the Persian Gulf nations, to name but a few. Asia's competitiveness also extends to metals, generic pharmaceuticals, and clinical research.

Asia's Technology Thrust

The wide range of IT-related skills and clusters in Asia is well known, so we will focus here on a cross-section of high-growth areas that several Asian economies have developed within this broad sphere. Telecommunications and related services, especially content delivery, is where the greatest growth is currently taking place across Asia, but consumer electronics too has emerged as a key growth area. The proliferation of personal computers, broadband Internet access and usage, along with very significant mobile-phone penetration is driving value addition and revenues for everyone from wireless-telecom operators, Internet-based businesses, online-gaming software producers, and hardware and electronics manufacturers.

Internet access and mobile-phone penetration are two of the biggest growth stories in recent years. Along with Japan and Korea, China is now growing to be Asia's leading market for broadband Internet and mobile telephony. China Telecom Corp. is a very big beneficiary of this fast growth in broadband Internet, which expands on its fixed-line offerings. As in India and other parts of the emerging world, where wireless telephony and wireless mobile applications have created a blazing growth trajectory, fixed-line growth is slow in China. Therefore it is China Mobile—the world's largest telecom company by market capitalization as well as by wireless subscribers—that will reap the real benefits. It is the convergence between wireless devices and the Internet, known as 3G (third-generation) wireless, which will create the greatest value for China Mobile. According to market-research group IDC, China's 3G mobile-phone subscribers will triple by 2010, to nearly 10 million from a little over three million in 2009, as wireless broadband begins to take off in China. The company, which has well over 500 million wireless subscribers (some 70 percent of the market), may not be the fastest of Chinese wireless companies to adopt new technologies, but it has the advantage of size, reliability, and the ability to roll out new technologies well. It is already planning to leverage its wireless-broadband capabilities with content tie-ups with China Broadcasting Corporation to promote television content on its network and introduce software that enables the downloading and reading of documents on mobile devices.

China's mobile-user base is rivaled only by India in scale and growth. Toward the third quarter of 2009 India had 450 million mobile subscribers, of whom Bharti Airtel, the largest Indian wireless company, had almost 120 million subscribers, and Reliance Communications had 90 million. Where China Mobile has a market cap of US$191 billion, Bharti Airtel's market cap is US$25 billion. To counter the severe, and in some cases debilitating, price wars in India's wireless market, leading Indian providers such as Bharti, Reliance, and Tata Teleservices have moved quickly to provide value-added services, including direct-to-home TV and wireless broadband through their affiliated companies. With the advent of bundled services, the potential in India is huge. Nearly 250 million households have TV sets and 70 million have cable TV. There are 20 million DTH TV subscribers, with the industry expecting to maintain the momentum for the next few years after adding a futher 10 million in 2009. Airtel TV has a quarter of a million new subscribers a month.

Animation and Gaming: The "Soft" Touch

While portions of the Asian Internet industry, especially search-related advertising revenues, have shrunk during the 2008–09 recession (though Korea is an exception) online-gaming revenues across markets have remained strong. Korean companies have proliferated in the online-gaming market, leveraging that country's significant Internet penetration and net-savvy population. Companies such as NCSoft Corporation dominate in a very competitive market. NCSoft has grown rapidly, with strong product introductions and reported revenues of US$220 million for 2008. Another interesting Korean play is Neowiz Games, which has built revenues of US$150 million, the bulk of which come from sales in China. It has also diversified its market to include Vietnam and Japan, and the pace of growth is likely to continue.

South Korea is one of the world's largest, most dynamic, and innovative e-commerce markets, and it came as no surprise that eBay eventually paid a decent premium to buy Gmarket, Korea's largest auction site, valuing the company in early 2009 at nearly US$2 billion.

Chinese companies too are beginning to reflect the growth derived from producing gaming software for their own markets and global investors are taking notice of that. According to some estimates, China's current online-gaming market size is US$4 billion and is expected to grow to US$11 billion by 2012 when it is expected to have 230 million gamers, compared to 69 million today. Changyou.com Ltd. (a subsidiary of Chinese Internet giant Sohu.com) provides a good example of what's happening. The Beijing-based company, which makes role-playing games for a Chinese audience, earned revenues of US$201 million in 2008 and made its stock market debut on the NASDAQ in April 2009 at a time of heightened market uncertainty. The outlook for the Chinese market and the company's operating strength was such that it could price the 7.5 million American Depository Shares at the top end of its expected US$14–16 price range. The stock gained 38 percent on its opening trade and ended its first day up 40 percent, making it the best performer since potash fertilizer manufacturer Intrepid Potash Inc. rose 58 percent on its debut a year earlier. Changyou eventually went on to return nearly 200 percent (a high price of US$48) within a couple of months of listing.

The gaming market in China is fragmented but that enables well-capitalized companies like Changyou to cut deals to co-develop and cross-market products, thus considerably shortening development cycles. The company has also begun to get the attention of smaller or single-product developers and therefore obtain rights to attractive suites of titles.

While Changyou.com has created a stir in the markets, it is well-established companies such as Tencent Holdings, Netease.com Inc., and Shanda Games Ltd. that epitomize the potential of China's online-gaming market. With a revenue base of US$400 million and a market cap in excess of US$5 billion, Netease has a far stronger operating history and balance sheet than Changyou. Tencent Holdings operates what is considered to be the most popular Internet portal in China, and its key offering is a free Internet messaging service, from which all its other offerings have emerged. Its foray into online games has pushed its growth rates significantly. The key to Tencent is its powerful portal-based services and huge pool of users.

The domestic operating environment is very positive for gaming companies in China, particularly in light of government prohibitions on certain types of content, which effectively restrict the offerings of foreign competitors. The other factor is that there is a large under-served and very young market for these games, and companies have the pricing power necessary to produce very decent margins (nearing 40 percent for companies like Changyou and Netease).

According to the National Association of Software and Services Companies (NASSCOM), the Indian IT industry association, the animation and gaming industries are witnessing a growth spurt. Revenues for the animation industry in India are estimated at US$500 million (a large portion of which comes from outsourcing) and are expected to grow to over US$1 billion by 2012. Similarly, the gaming industry, which currently stands at less than US$200 million, is expected to gain momentum in growing to more than US$800 million by 2012.

The combination of rapid Internet penetration, local-language content, low cost of usage, and booming consumer economies makes China, Korea, and Taiwan very attractive markets for online information search companies. Companies such as NHN Corp., the largest Korean Internet company (search engine and online gaming) and third-largest in Asia (after Baidu Inc. and Alibaba.com Ltd.), have grown very fast. Even though revenues have been hit by advertising cutbacks in 2008 and 2009, NHN has strong core businesses and is very well capitalized. NHN, which recorded revenues of US$1.2 billion for 2008, has grown revenues by nearly 50 percent annually over a five-year period, is nearly debt free, and has almost 40 percent of its assets in cash or liquid investments. China Real Estate Information Corp., which is listed on the NASDAQ Global Select market, is another company riding this combination. It offers basic and value-added information services in the Chinese real-estate sector but its real potential stems from Internet usage and its online brand and service offerings. China TransInfo Technology Corp., a leading provider of public transportation information-systems technology and comprehensive solutions in China, is another to look out for. The company also provides electronic toll-collection systems and has already won contracts to install roadside antennas and sensors in Shandong and Zhejiang provinces.

Baidu Inc. is one of the top Chinese companies in online search and has beaten Google at the game in China. Baidu commands almost 70 percent of the Chinese search market and has a strong competitive edge in its understanding of local Chinese culture and preferences that Google Inc. has not been able to match. Google, however, has a vastly improved presence in China and remains a formidable threat to Baidu, which has been almost doubling its revenues every year for the past five years but remains just one-twentieth the size of Google. Google too continues to grow at a frantic pace, with a 70 percent five-year compounded growth in revenues. The single biggest threat to Baidu's growth plans comes from Google's mobile search applications. While Baidu has a clear lead in Internet search, Google has managed to get its Android mobile search application installed on China Mobile's 3G phones, while Baidu has struck a deal with second- and third-place carriers China Unicom and China Telecom. But as we have seen, China Mobile has a very significant size advantage over the other two, giving Google a huge head start in the mobile search market in China. If Google were to withdraw from China, it would significantly enhance the value of Baidu.

Alibaba.com Ltd., another interesting bet on China's huge emerging Web marketplace, is China's largest business-to-business (B2B) portal, most of whose revenue is derived from Chinese exporters. It has several million registered clients and facilitates Chinese trade in three broad sectors: within China, with Japan, and globally. This company has recorded a 58 percent compound growth in revenues over the five-year period ending in 2008. It has a very strong balance sheet, with nearly 90 percent of its assets in cash and short-term investments, and is completely debt free. The company continued to make significant investments in its Internet trading platform and in growing its franchise through multi-lingual services and additional marketing. Annualized revenues have crossed US$400 million, and, following a hugely successful IPO, the company is still sitting on a cash pile of over US$1 billion.

Software Services: Almost Recession-Proof

While India too is seeing a growth spurt in its Internet-related businesses, the lower levels of PC penetration mean that the market is smaller. The growth rates are not comparable to those in East Asia, and the choice of investment names is still limited. However, it is the much-vaunted Indian software-services companies that remain the backbone of the Indian IT industry. Over a 20-year period beginning in 1990, the Indian software industry has grown from US$175 million in (largely export) revenues to US$41 billion in export revenues and US$24 billion in domestic revenues, with an annual growth rate of 37 percent. The evolution of a potentially strong and vibrant domestic market for outsourced software and business-process outsourcing (BPO) services is a trend consistent with those unfolding in the rest of Asia, where the domestic market is absorbing the capacities and capabilities created to cater to the rest of the world, which continues to remain a very viable growth market for Indian software services and BPO companies.

Despite strong free cash flows, unleveraged balance sheets, and nearly two decades of uninterrupted growth, Indian software-services giants were slow to move up the value chain. There are only a handful of Indian companies like i-Flex Solutions Ltd. that have been very successful in developing products for the global market. But the larger ones that have created strong global brand equity have established successful consulting practices.

With their sophisticated delivery models complemented by strong service capabilities and programming skills, however, it is unlikely that India's IT companies will be challenged by other countries in the near future, despite the fact that Israel and Ireland have built up some expertise and scale in this industry. Indian software-services companies are among the world's largest services companies, are extremely competitive, and well positioned for acquisitions. This is especially true of Infosys, which has been very conservative in its acquisitions despite its very aggressive growth rates. Wipro Technologies has been more aggressive with its acquisition strategy and is very likely to continue with its growth trajectory. Among the better emerging IT-services companies in India is 3i Infotech. As corporations worldwide increase their capital expenditure cycle on hardware and systems that will automatically also boost their software services requirements, this should offer a boost to Indian software services and outsourcing companies.

Hardware

Currently the penetration of personal computers is very low in Asia, even in the fast-emerging markets of China and India. In China, for example, industry research shows that the total penetration of PCs is just 12 percent and is expanding at double-digit growth rates. Given that East Asia is the manufacturing hub for electronic parts, critical assemblies, and even complete TVs and monitors, the full impact of this increased PC and electronics penetration in Asia will be seen in Asian companies.

Led by China, Asia has been quick to absorb technology, and the rapid growth in PCs, flat-screen TVs, mobile phones, and LCD display has been well documented. However, Asia has yet to reach a critical mass for several of these products for markets outside of China. As the cost of hardware continues to fall and as national governments begin to emulate the Chinese model and push hard for more widespread technology absorption, the case for hardware growth in Asia becomes more solid. There is a vast array of Asian and global companies that can benefit from these core trends.

The key trends are in mobile phones, smart phones, and new-generation TV sets and displays. As noted earlier, it is telecommunications that is growing very rapidly and evenly across most Asian nations. Samsung Electronics has a product range that stretches across the consumer and geographic spectrum, including a wide range of consumer electronics, semiconductors, Internet-access network systems, mobile phones, and home appliances. Samsung is better positioned than most in that it is leveraged to developed economies and also has a strong exposure to emerging Asia, which it is pursuing for incremental growth. The company is a very competitive manufacturer of these goods and is likely to maintain that edge.

Chi Mei Optoelectronics Corp. is a Taiwanese manufacturer of thin-film transistor LCD panels and color filters and is comparable to South Korea's LG Display Co. Ltd., which is one of the largest display manufacturers in the world with annual revenues in 2008 of US$15 billion (2008). The company was acquired by Innolux Display Corp., the world's third-largest display manufacturer.

ZTE Corporation, a large Chinese developer of high-tech hardware that includes switches, access servers, video conferencing, and mobile communications systems, is a strong growth candidate. In addition to its exposure to the Chinese market, ZTE is also a major contender for the supply of hardware to the India 3G rollout, which will be another very significant development for the Asian broadband, mobile telephony, and content markets. HTC, a Taiwanese handset manufacturer and one of Asia's better-known technology brands, is also likely to be a major beneficiary from these evolving trends. Taiwanese chip maker Mediatek Inc. will benefit from orders from China Mobile for its 3G handsets. Mediatek is an extremely profitable company with an average five-year RoE of 36 percent and total revenues of nearly US$ 2.5 billion (five-year average sales growth of 12 percent). China Mobile 3G handsets are unique in the sense that they are based on technology developed in China, unlike its rivals China Unicom and China Telecom that use global 3G technology. Similarly, Datang Telecom, one of the major hardware manufacturers in China, will help China Mobile with its mobile-reader services.

The 3G convergence and smartphone phenomenon has also come at an opportune time for Asia's strong contingent of touch-screen manufacturing companies, based largely in Taiwan, Korea, and Japan. To date, the industry is fragmented, and though there are some listed entities in these countries and the US, these are generally very small and untested in a small but fast-growing industry. The potential for a large number of competitors emerging is very real. Much of the technology development has taken place in Canada and the US, so the Asian manufacturers will be, to a large extent, technology licensors. A few companies that have shown recent profitability trends are PixArt from Taiwan and Digitech and ELK from Korea.

From Low-Cost Manufacturing to Value-Added Manufacturing

Asian corporations now understand the need to integrate globally, not just at the product end but in the sourcing of raw materials or acquiring companies overseas for technology and best practices.

Asian companies have integrated themselves firmly with the global economy over decades and in many industries have become essential to global supply chains with their low-cost manufacturing and global-delivery capability both in goods and services. This knowledge and experience now gives Asian companies a serious competitive advantage as they position themselves to benefit from growing economic integration within Asia. But even though low cost remains a core element of Asia's competitive edge, a spirit of innovation has taken root in a few industries. As Asian companies have started to move up the value chain there is clear evidence of research collaboration between companies and universities, leading to breakthroughs in nanotechnology, semiconductor manufacturing, robotics, chemicals, and biotechnology.

The scale and depth of the auto industry in China and India are clear signs of how much emerging Asia's manufacturing prowess has grown and how far it has come by way of technological advancement. Though China largely consumes most of its own auto production, India exports a sizeable quantity of its auto and component output. Indian manufacturing in this industry was honed by nearly two decades of excess capacity and cut-throat domestic competition, which forced companies to upgrade and build markets outside the country. Indian manufacturers today have a wider and deeper market for their production across the globe than their Chinese counterparts.

Incredible as it may seem, in certain industries such as consumer electronics, it seems that the only manufacturers of any consequence left are Asian multinational companies such as Sony, Samsung, LG, Haier, Fujitsu, Toshiba, and so on. Many, if not all, of these companies are accessible to investors the world over, since they have multiple listings in either London or New York, in addition to their home markets. This raises the question as to whether they remain truly Asian companies, especially since there have been significant amalgamations of different business units with European or American companies (LG Electronics, for example, merged its LCD business with Philips several years ago). This being the case, while they are exposed to Asian growth, they are also exposed to economic weakness elsewhere in the world and to very significant currency risks. While we acknowledge the formidable presence of such companies in their respective sectors, we would do well to look for the Asia-based suppliers of intermediate electronics or domestic manufacturers and marketers in these segments. The likes of ZTE Corp, Huawei, Datang Telecom, and HTC epitomize how Asian companies have learned from the West and moved up the value chain to become formidable competitors even to Western giants such as Lucent or Cisco Systems. Also, the fact that global giants such as Texas Instruments, Intel, Siemens, Nokia, and Motorola have made large R&D and manufacturing investments in China and India means that sooner of later the technological impetus will be felt across local industry, as happened with automobiles in Japan or software services in India (where companies like IBM seeded the concept).

High-technology manufacturing in Israel is a clear example of the competitive advantage that is so inherent in Asia. There are a number of high-technology, hardware and software clusters in Israel. The competitive advantage that Israel possesses is the high quality of its manpower. Israeli government support for this industry is spectacular; one of the programs that the Israeli government runs is a technology incubator program where entrepreneurs with ideas can get the funding they need to develop products and establish the necessary development facilities. According to Israeli government statistics, the country possesses 135 engineers per 10,000 people, which is one of the highest concentrations in the world. Israel's strength in defense technology and manufacturing is one of its greatest sources of competitive advantage in the software industry, with thousands of engineers working on cutting-edge systems and technology in avionics, aerospace technologies, advanced materials, computing technology, and electronics.

Despite advances with branded products and high-tech successes, Asia's edge in low-cost manufacturing is omnipresent. As innocuous a product as shoes is probably Asia's signature outsourced product, with manufacturers dispersed across the continent. Yue Yuen Industrial Holdings Ltd. epitomizes this very Asian phenomenon. The company is the world's largest manufacturer of athletic shoes, with revenues of nearly US$5 billion for the year ending September 2008. The company has nearly 40 years of operating history, with Taiwanese ownership, a Hong Kong listing, production facilities in China, Indonesia, and Vietnam, and sales networks throughout Asia, Europe, and North America. Where once almost all its revenues originated from sales to US brands, sales from within Asia now account for one-third of the total. In 2006 the US market accounted for 40 percent of its revenues, which dropped to 31 percent by 2008. China's role in the company's operation is changing very significantly: where once it was used to simply manufacture the product it has now become Yue Yuen's fastest-growing market. In 2008–09, revenues from China have increased by 74 percent, while consolidated revenues for the company were up 19 percent. In some quarters, growth from China reached 100 percent. Needless to say, its focus now is the Greater China region, and Asia will probably become a significant source of its revenues. The company has already begun to push its China presence and increased the number of its stores—both directly owned and through joint ventures—from 3,000 at the end of 2006 to 4,700 at the end of 2008. In addition, wholesale distribution points in China have increased from 2,600 to 2,900, giving the company almost unparalleled access to the Chinese market. The company's retailing approach has been to create a mix of single- and multi-brand stores as well as sporting goods stores, thus taking it beyond just shoes. Despite this level of penetration, the company still considers the Chinese footwear market to be in its infancy. While this company once epitomized the China outsourcing story, it is now very much a China growth story.

A good example of high-quality manufacturing and technological and process excellence is in India's flexible packaging industry where companies such as Paper Products Ltd. and Essel Propack Ltd. dominate and supply almost the entire premium packaging requirements of companies such as Colgate, Unilever, Nestlé, P&G, Cadbury, and a variety of other domestic and multinational corporations.

Domestic Defense Manufacturing

India's defense industry is planning an investment of US$100 billion over the next few years in equipment acquisitions, mainly in aerospace. Foreign aerospace suppliers will be required to sub-contract or manufacture 30 percent of the components through India's aerospace industry. India also has a few listed companies that actively cater to the defense sector. Though China has a larger defense-manufacturing sector, particularly in aircraft and avionics, all of the companies involved are state-owned. Sooner or later, some of these companies will tap the capital markets, especially as the large number of domestic manufacturers consolidate and seek to acquire companies overseas—something that will be incredibly difficult for any purely state-owned entity to achieve. The 2009 takeover of the Austrian parts-manufacturer Future Advanced Composite Components AG by Xi'an Aircraft Industry Group is a case in point. The company now plans to merge most of its assets into a Shenzhen-listed subsidiary and raise nearly US$700 million in an IPO in 2010.

In an attempt to promote a private defense industry, Indian defense scientists will be allowed to benefit from technological breakthroughs made in national defense laboratories. Most of the defense companies listing in the public markets have been promoted by former defense scientists. Astra Microwave is one such company: founded by Defense Research and Development Organization (DRDO) scientists, it is now part of several defense-related projects. Other Indian companies in this field include Bharat Electronics and Larsen & Toubro.

Metals and Mining

Asia's mastery of the commodities cycle now has changed to domination as Asian nations increasingly acquire raw material sources and, with a growing emphasis on research and development, brand building, and modern management practices, move up the value chain, especially in mine productivity and metals production.

Asian nations now possess the greatest capacities for processing all types of industrial and agricultural commodities, from cotton to iron ore to high-grade aluminum and rare earth minerals. It is no coincidence that along with Asia's capacity additions and ownership of mineral resources across the world it has also witnessed the birth and growth of commodity exchanges in a big way. Shanghai and Mumbai have become key players in the global commodities scene. Shanghai has become the key arbiter of industrial commodities, while India sets the tone in a number of agricultural commodities and has a thriving market in industrial commodities, gold, and oil and gas-linked derivative contracts. India has so far resisted the attraction of allowing foreigners into its commodity markets, but when it does the scale and sophistication that has been built will make it a force in the global commodities market.

A study by the Bank of Canada in 2007–08 showed that the price of commodities, including oil, was historically influenced by economic cycles in the developed world, especially the West. However, since 1997 that causal relationship has broken down; commodity prices and demand patterns are now heavily influenced by consumption and industrial-demand patterns in emerging Asia, especially China. The demand for commodities tends to accelerate once per-capita income reaches between US$5,000–10,000 per annum (China is at US$3,500 and India at US$1,000), so there is considerable room for growth in both demand and prices.

As China continues to invest in its domestic economy, as the pace of investment picks up in India, and as economic integration between major emerging Asian nations also gathers pace, the demand for commodities and its impact on prices will be quite significant. Investing in natural-resource companies within or outside of Asia or directly in commodities is a great way to gain exposure to growth in Asia. As a caveat, though, events in 2008 and 2009 have shown that even this most obvious of strategies can be extremely risky when both demand and price collapse.

It makes sense to focus on those commodities which are essential in large quantities for infrastructure creation and for new, rapidly growing technologies. Base metals such as steel and copper, iron ore, coal, and metallurgical coal (coking coal) are critical elements for a developing world. Fuel for nuclear-powered plants and rare earth minerals will become increasingly more important to the global investment community. Plans for the addition of nuclear-power generating capacity around the world is almost unprecedented (China, Korea, and India are major contributors in this), which brings uranium mining into focus.

While the Kazakh mining company Kazatomprom is on track to become the world's largest uranium miner, it is Canada that produces nearly one-quarter of the world's uranium requirements, and which, along with Australian mining companies, can benefit most from sharp demand growth and price increases. India is focusing on the development of thorium as an alternative to uranium as a source of nuclear fuel. It has 90 percent of known deposits of thorium and is committed to developing technologies around it. The Indian nuclear establishment is already working on the development of an Advanced Heavy Water Reactor based on a thorium fuel cycle.

The mining of rare earth metals (REMs), which are critical for making the high-technology components needed for hybrid cars, wind-turbine generators, and many other products, is coming into focus too. Rare earth metals, as their name implies, are found in minis-cule quantities (economic mining operations need a certain level of mineral concentration) in the Earth's surface. The ideal concentra-tion for economic mining of these minerals has been found only in the US, China, India, Australia, Brazil, and Malaysia to date. However, Kazakhstan and Vietnam are emerging as a potential destination for rare-earth investments, and Japanese companies such as Showa Denko, Toyota Motors, (which is looking for stable supplies for its hybrid and electric-car development program) and Sumitomo Corp. are active investors in Vietnam. According to the US Geological Survey, how-ever, China accounts for 96 percent of the world's production of REMs, giving it a virtual monopoly over materials that will drive the future world. Among the world's leading producers is Inner Mongolia Baotou Steel Rare-Earth Hi-Tech Co. There are a number of other emerging players in Australia, China, and Canada but these are smaller companies that are as yet untested. The refiners of REMs include Molycorp, a subsidiary of Chevron Inc. in the US, which refines REM ores and produces rare earth minerals and intermediaries, and French company Rhodia.

Even as nuclear energy is being contemplated seriously, most Asian nations are racing to bridge the energy gap in their respective coun-tries with coal-fired power plants. Both India and China are among the world's top five producers and consumers of coal. The Energy Information Administration (EIA), which is a part of the US Department of Energy (DoE), has projected that from 2006 until 2030, 90 percent of the projected increase in world coal consumption will come from emerg-ing Asian nations, especially China, India, and Indonesia, and most of the increased demand for power will be met through coal.

Given the projected rise in consumption and corresponding invest-ments needed in mines and transportation infrastructure, a number of mining IPOs or even cross-border industry consolidation can be expected. One of the biggest IPOs expected to come out of India in 2010 is that of Coal India Ltd., the country's largest coal producer. The Coal India IPO should bring a very large and interesting player into the markets, but right now the top players to consider are Chinese companies China Shenhua and China Coal, and two Indonesian producers, Bumi Resources and Adaro Energy. China Shenhua is one of the world's largest coal producers, with revenues of US$15 billion and market capitalization of US$105 billion, making it an expensive sector play priced on par with Rio Tinto and BHP Billiton and a well-integrated mining, coal transportation, and thermal power-generation business.

Iron-ore producers such as Sesa Goa will be huge beneficiaries of the continued development of Asia. Coking-coal producer Gujarat NRE Coke is a company that will ride the price push to coking coal, which, in turn, is a key cost driver of steel. The steel industry in Asia has grown by leaps in the past 20 years, with almost all the world's new capacity coming up in a few emerging Asian economies. Tata Steel, POSCO, Baoshan Iron & Steel, Angang Steel, and Wuhan Iron and Steel Corp., to name a few, are now among the leading integrated steel players. Vedanta Plc is one of the lowest-cost producers of zinc and copper in the world. Vedanta stands out as a classic growth story; starting out as a metal trader in India, in the space of 15 years it has grown into a major integrated global metals player. The company's initial growth spurt came from successfully bidding for public-sector metal companies that were auctioned off by the Indian government, and it has built a strong global presence in the last decade. It is likely to bid for other large metals and mining companies that become available as part of the Indian government's renewed focus on privatization.

Several engineering- and mining-equipment producers are well poised to capitalize on the huge investments that are being generated by the demand for metals, coal, and other ores. Hong Kong-listed Sany Heavy Equipment International, a leading manufacturer of coal-mining equipment in China, is a good example.

A record (but eventually unsuccessful) acquisition attempt by a Chinese company in early 2009 showed the sustained importance that China places on commodities and the likely direction that it expects prices to go. Chinalco, the largest aluminum company in China, attempted to invest US$19.5 billion in global mining giant Rio Tinto. The investment was to be made in a combination of US$7.2 billion convertibles and US$12.3 billion in a collection of mining assets spread across Chile, Australia, and the US, which would have given the company a stronger grip on key mining assets across the world, especially valuable copper mines in Chile. While Rio Tinto backed out of the deal, it is very likely that we will hear of many more attempts by the Chinese to buy out mining assets wherever they can find them.

The fallout from the stressed economic environment of 2008−09 is providing more opportunities for cash-rich buyers to increase their stakes in mining companies and mining regions. A key factor driving Chinese acquisitions is their access to funding. The funding for Chinalco's bid for a stake in Rio Tinto would have come from a consortium of Chinese banks led by the central bank offering to finance the deal at well below market rates (reportedly at a minimal spread over six-month Libor). China Minmetals' acquisition of Australia's OZ group for US$1.2 billion and its investments in Teck Cominco of Canada is another example of this trend. The acquisition of physical assets is also a way for the Chinese to hedge their massive US$2 trillion in foreign-exchange reserves.

Companies such as Woodside Petroleum Ltd. (WPL) could be beneficiaries of Chinese investments in LNG projects in Australia. Though Woodside has a significant exposure to Japan, it is otherwise well diversified geographically.

Chapter 5

Asia: The Next Great Financial Supermarket

The contagion years of 2007–2009 devastated most of the world's financial industry, but, with the exception of Japan's financial sector and Dubai's real-estate sector (which suffered for different reasons), Asian economies experienced banking, monetary, and, to a large extent, currency stability and saw the further development of cross-border trade in financial services. The evolution of such trade is likely to result in the emergence of pan-Asian banking, insurance, and asset-management brands, an approach epitomized by Singapore's 70-year-old United Overseas Bank. The bank has more than 500 branches across the Asia-Pacific region, Europe, and North America and is involved in a every aspect of financial services (though it may sell its life insurance subsidiary to a larger Asian or global player). It is also becoming firmly entrenched in Chinese banking and Korean asset-management segments.

The evolution of the financial sector is crucial to the growth and well-being of the Asian economic system. Among the key trends driving the emergence of the sector are favorable demographics for mortgages and credit cards, a huge growing market in wealth management, a high savings rate, the increasing sophistication of markets and investors, and the emergence of new consumer-oriented banks, insurance companies, and asset managers.

Consumer loans, mortgages, insurance, and asset management, therefore, are key growth areas. Mortgages as a percentage of GDP is small: in China it is 12 percent; India, 7 percent; Indonesia, 2 percent, Thailand, 16 percent; even in Japan it is around 10 percent. Whether the penetration levels will ever get to the 70–80 percent of GDP that we have seen in the US and other Western economies is hard to say; but what is certain is that there is a fast-growing market for mortgages. In India, for example, the Housing Development Finance Corporation (HDFC) is seeing a 25 percent annual growth in mortgages. The other listed specialist residential mortgage companies in India such as LIC Housing Finance are also seeing very strong growth rates. In other parts of emerging Asia there are no such specialist companies, and it is the large commercial banks that service this market. Among the Indian banks, State Bank of India, ICICI Bank, and Axis Bank have built a considerable portfolio of mortgages, which, for the most part, is of excellent quality, with an average loan-to-value ratio of below 70 percent.

It is the asset-management segment that will see rapid growth across Asia and where there is likely to be cross-border activity. India's asset-management industry has grown at 50 percent for the past few years, and, according to a McKinsey & Co. estimate, it can continue growing at 30–35 percent a year driven equally by institutional and retail activity. By 2009 the industry had grown to US$125 billion and expects to be in the region of US$460–500 billion by 2015. So in just a few years it is expected to grow from 12 percent to 30 percent of GDP, which is where China and Korea are at present. The US is roughly at 80 percent. But, more importantly, while 15–33 percent of households in the developed market own mutual funds, in India this figure stands at less than 3 percent, and less than 1 percent have brokerage accounts.

Reliance Capital Ltd. is the largest private asset-management company in India and the only one that is not a joint venture with a global fund house. The company has US$18 billion in assets under management and its pedigree and performance have ensured tremendous brand equity among Indian investors. Its latest fund offering raised an unprecedented US$1.3 billion from almost a million domestic investors.

India and China are now seen as major emerging markets for financial services, and China's 2001 accession to the WTO has hastened the global trade in financial services. The opportunities for investors in China's financial-services sector may be unprecedented in scope and size. The fund-management industry, for example, has become one of China's most open sectors for foreign competitors. Where in 1998 there were just 10 active asset-management companies, managing less than US$70 billion, now there are almost 60 companies (of which half represent overseas companies), with nearly US$340 billion under management. This asset pool is expected to grow to US$1 trillion by 2014.

The size of the opportunity in these countries can be seen in the context of the large annual savings rate across Asia, where every US$1 trillion in GDP produces in the region of US$300–400 billion in annual savings. Between 50 percent and 70 percent of these savings accumulate in banks or government-run savings products largely geared toward buying real estate. So far, almost all real estate has been financed with savings, but once the mortgage concept or the use of variable annuities as an alternative savings tool is better understood the proportion of household assets allocated to the capital markets will increase exponentially. South Koreans are very net-savvy and there is such a degree of penetration that, married with its high degree of financial integration, they are the leaders in online stock trading (which incidentally also makes Korean markets very volatile). Korea has a number of financial names among its large and well-capitalized brokers and insurance companies, such as Daewoo Securities and Samsung Fire & Marine Insurance, a top-tier property and casualty insurer, available to foreign investors.

It is in the banking sector that the greatest changes have happened: for example, over 250 foreign banks, many of which are regional players, have either opened multiple branches or have set up representative offices in China. The Chinese financial sector itself can produce major regional players as the Chinese government has permitted 40 banks, insurance companies, and asset-management companies to expand overseas, mainly in Asia.

Insurance: A Premium Sector

The near-death experience of AIG in 2008 raised the curtain on the value of Asia's insurance sector to global insurance companies. Insurance companies worldwide girded themselves for battle in anticipation that AIG would eventually have to sell its stake in many of its subsidiaries in the US, Europe, and Asia, and it was AIG's Asian businesses that were most coveted. The reason for the anticipated rush for access to the Asian insurance market is that Asia is underinsured, with low penetration rates. Growth rates across emerging Asian markets are 30–35 percent per annum. Despite rapid growth, insurance assets to GDP stand at 4 percent in India, 8 percent in South Korea, 9 percent in Japan, 13 percent in the UK, and 15 percent in the US. Once again, it is China and India that are at the epicenter of the global insurance industry's enthusiasm for Asia. China now has the world's largest bank and the world's largest insurance company by market capitalization; China Life. Other leading insurance companies in China are Ping An and China Taiping Insurance Holdings (CTIH), which offers everything from life, property, and casualty insurance to wealth management. People's Insurance Company of China (PICC), which is largely a property and casualty insurer, has the necessary scale and reach but has still to demonstrate meaningful balance-sheet and operational strength before it can be seriously considered to be worthy of investment. PICC is also partly owned by AIG. Yuanta Financial Holding Co. is a Taiwan-based pan-Asian financial conglomerate with strong regional insurance subsidiaries. Cathay Financial Holding Co. is another strong player but is focused on the Taiwanese insurance and securities market.

The main source of concern for North American and European insurers is also that of Asian insurers; that is, the distinct possibility of a low interest-rate regime, which could impede their medium-term investment return assumptions and trigger a reduction in earnings and valuation. This is important because, though there are significant growth opportunities and limited competition, the great run-up in Chinese insurers from October 2008 until the third quarter of 2009, where insurers' returns reached 120 percent, means that a lot of the value has already been acknowledged and insurers have used the period of uncertainty to recapitalize. In addition, Chinese and other Asian insurers still offer more traditional endowment products rather than the universal life and variable annuity (also known as unit-linked insurance products or ULIPs) that are more popular with insurers in the US and Canada. As investors become more sophisticated, the demand for ULIPs is bound to increase, driving earnings of the better-capitalized insurance companies.

India, one of the fastest-growing insurance markets in the world, has developed an agent-based selling model from the very beginning; even the public-sector companies that long dominated the sector used agents on a large scale. The spate of voluntary retirement schemes in Indian public-sector banks in the 1990s produced a deep pool of experienced bankers from which the newly liberalizing Indian insurance industry created a huge base of agents. In China, the model thus far has been different and has relied for the most part on bancassurance sales (cross-selling through banking channels). Chinese insurance companies have recently made the move to an agent-based sales model, which is producing stupendous growth in the number of policies written and is linked to the furious pace at which new agents are being recruited. China Life is comparable in a sense with the Life Insurance Corporation of India (unlisted and owned entirely by the Indian government) in that, despite the rising sophistication of the market and the customers, it continues to focus on plain-vanilla endowment products in which it holds the edge despite the entrance of sophisticated and well-capitalized competitors. The private-sector entrants into India's life business since the sector was opened in the late 1990s have shaken up the stodgy image of insurance policies in India from a predominantly savings-oriented product to a risk-mitigation instrument.

Unlike in China and other regional Asian markets, there are no publicly traded life insurers in India. Large, very fast-growing, and valuable insurance franchises do exist but they are all part of larger financial conglomerates (such as ICICI Bank's insurance joint venture with Prudential of the UK) or industrial groups (such as Birla's insurance joint venture with Sun Life of Canada), and direct exposure to the Indian insurance industry is difficult right now. The Indian regulators require at least a 10-year track record (since that is more or less the timeframe required to test the assumptions underlying insurance companies' embedded values). However, it is widely anticipated that sooner or later these conglomerates or large banks will want to unlock some of the value in their insurance subsidiaries by opting to list. All of the Indian private-sector insurance companies have joint ventures with large global life insurers, and, as we have seen in other sectors, a number of global names will be available to domestic and foreign investors.

Saudi Arabia is attempting a massive transformation of its healthcare market, which is likely to lead to the large-scale development of the private health-insurance industry. Currently, the entire Saudi healthcare industry, from hospitals to drug stores, is in the public sector and is tightly controlled. The Saudis are seeking to transfer the burden of providing healthcare, including the cost of prescription drugs of private-sector employees, to their employers. The government is also seeking to privatize hospitals. There are a number of health-insurance and financial-services stocks listed on stock exchanges in Abu Dhabi, Dubai, and Riyadh, most of which are former state-owned companies that are now in the process of being privatized.

Pan-Asian Institutional Infrastructure

Key lessons were learned during the Asian crisis of 1997–98, when part of the reason for the collapse of Asian currencies was the lack of concerted government action to provide liquidity to the currency markets and the lack of a cohesive regional focus on cross-currency support. Following that experience, East Asian economies decided to create a pool of common reserves that they can draw on to protect regional currencies in danger of becoming unstable. In recent months, led by China, the pool of reserves was increased to US$120 billion, which will make available a sizeable pool of financial resources to relieve any large speculative selling pressure that may arise against any of their currencies.

Unlike the other East Asian economies, Indonesia is not a manufacturing powerhouse and it is dependent on its natural-resource exports. These were hit by both falling demand and falling prices, threatening its currency and prompting Japan to provide government guarantees on any yen-denominated bonds that it may issue. South Korea and Singapore did see some weakening in their currencies but that was resolved with a bilateral deal with the US. The Asian bond market too has emerged as a recognized force in global finance. Since the Asian currency and banking crisis a stable and growing market has emerged for local-currency denominated Asian bonds. The market (excluding Japan) has been measured at US$43 trillion. With the weakening of the US dollar and the credit uncertainty in the US and Europe there is an even better platform for the Asian bond market to develop. We have already begun to see cross-border investment in government securities; for example, Thai bond funds invested US$15 billion in Korean government bonds in 2009. Thai investors found that despite the similarity in sovereign ratings Korean government bonds were trading at a higher yield. We are also probably moving closer to the creation of a Dragon bond market on the lines of the Yankee, Euro, and Samurai bond markets.

Now that there is momentum being built up in Asian banking, asset-management, and capital markets, the question being asked in Asian financial circles is whether the possibility exists for an Asian common currency. The short answer is that, given the complexities involved in creating the necessary cohesion in political and economic policy, this will probably not happen for a very long time.

As the seven nations of the GCC seek to strengthen cooperation between them there is also a concerted effort to form a common currency and a common Gulf Arab central bank that will drive regional monetary policy. This has its advantages and will eventually provide a fillip to a common regional capital market, which would rival in depth the leading capital markets in the world. Taken with the efforts to develop some key regional cities (Dubai, Doha, Manama, and Abu Dhabi) as regional financial centers, monetary union would certainly be a major milestone. However, regional rivalries are so intense that, while not rejecting the idea outright, some key states have given the idea only a lukewarm embrace. Whatever the outcome of the union slated for after 2010 it remains a good idea, especially if it leads to greater financial discipline and more transparency in those economies.

Chinese Banks: Asia's Achilles' Heel?

The year 2009 could turn out to be a major inflection point for China's four or five behemoth banks. China's massive economic stimulus of more than half a trillion US dollars and its unprecedented financial support to businesses mean that Chinese banks are being called upon to provide for the critical credit needs of the economy at very nominal terms. In a broader sense, the entire shift to move the Chinese economy from being driven by external markets to being driven by internal consumption is being enabled with inexpensive funding from Chinese banks. Being largely government-controlled, the banks have little choice but to comply with state directives to keep pumping liquidity into the economy. This single factor alone is likely to drive superlative earnings growth at Chinese banks.

However, there is a dark side to this unprecedented growth in domestic credit. Sooner or later, the Chinese banking system may well come under very significant stress, with large non-performing loans (NPLs) eventually surfacing. The probability of a higher level of NPLs for China's banks may alter the risk perception and investors will have to keep a keen eye out for how these banks navigate through the next few years. The Chinese banking system is two-tiered, with five large government-controlled banks—Industrial and Commercial Bank of China (ICBC), which is the largest bank in the world by market capitalization; China CITIC Bank; China Construction Bank; Bank of China; and the Agricultural Bank of China—and about a dozen other banks. As these top banks are likely to be protected by the government, the systemic risk may well come from the others.

Much of the overseas acquisition attempted by Chinese companies, especially in the resource sector, is also being funded on very nominal terms by Chinese banks. This is one very significant reason why Chinese companies can outbid any other global competitor for assets they want since cost of capital is something they do not have to worry about. But the banks lending the money will be forced to take cognizance of this at some point. More worrying for the moment is the distinct possibility of an asset bubble forming in China as liquidity looms large and cheap credit pours into real and financial assets. While mortgage penetration may be low, the real-estate exposure of Chinese banks is massive. The housing boom is financed with massive loans to property-development companies and to corporations seeking exposure to rapidly rising real-estate prices. Many medium-sized Chinese corporations facing severe export slowdowns are still eligible to borrow from the banks and are using this cheap source of capital to create an alternative source of income. For now, it seems, there is a debt-financed real-estate bubble looming in China. How long the banking boom or the asset bubble will last is anybody's guess. However, at some point this growing euphoria will have to be dealt with.

Chinese capital ratios are currently adequate by global standards, especially for the larger banks. However, with a compound average growth of 20 percent expected in Chinese bank assets for the next three or four years, these ratios are likely to come under a lot of stress. It is very likely that China's banks will have to raise a great deal of capital to shore up both their Tier I and Tier II ratios. Global institutional investors will find it hard to accept Chinese bank bonds without these banks raising more equity capital first. It is quite likely that 2010–11 will see a number of Chinese banks attempting to raise equity capital. At the time of writing, the Chinese government had already become wary of the rapid acceleration in credit and asset formation and had begun to prod banks to think about raising additional capital, especially core or equity capital as opposed to debt. Chinese banks had already begun to securitize some of their loans and thereby reduce pressure on capital and liquidity and create more room to lend without having to actually raise capital. But because the securitization transactions are not very transparent (since banks are not obliged to report them), the banks and other institutions could easily end up holding asset-backed securities that could be of dubious quality, leading to a contagion-like effect somewhere down the line.

Foreign investors seeking exposure to China, especially through indexed funds or exchange-traded funds (ETFs), are significantly and inadvertently exposed to Chinese banks since they are all listed in Hong Kong and make up around 57 percent of that market's Hang Seng Index and the Hang Seng China Enterprises Index. In late 2009, when the Chinese bank regulator hinted at tougher standards for capital adequacy in light of unprecedented loan growth and growth in an opaque securitization market, banks fell between 8–10 percent in a single day. The entire market fell by 4–5 percent as a result of the excess weight that banks have in total market capitalization. In India, by comparison, the entire financial sector has a 23 percent weight and is very tightly regulated.

An index gaining in popularity among global investment funds is the MSCI Golden Dragon index, which tracks stocks in the Greater China region (covering China, Hong Kong, and Taiwan), more than 35 percent of which are in financials, mostly mainland Chinese banks. There are a number of ETFs and mutual funds such as the China Opportunities Fund offered by MFC Global Investment Management, and the China Investment Fund Inc., managed by Martin Curie Inc., which track these indices and provide exposure to these rapidly growing sectors. For now, at least, Chinese banks remain intimately supported and controlled by the government. In the current economic climate this is clearly a good thing, and, taken along with the insularity of the Chinese financial system, it indicates relative strength and stability and provides comfort to those seeking exposure to the Chinese economy and financial system. A classic example of how the banking system works in China is the Agricultural Bank of China (Agbank). The Agbank is used by the Chinese government to prop up the agriculture center with soft financing to hundreds of millions of farmers. Over the years, the bank has picked up a large number of non-performing loans and in early 2009 obtained a US$19 billion cash injection from the government so that it could continue to support the agricultural sector. After the recapitalization, the bank's social and agricultural lending policy function has been vested in other entities, and the Agbank now functions as one of China's top-tier commercial banks.

Similar banking structures that aid social objectives also exist in India, but there, unlike China, banks have to compete very hard in what is essentially a very fragmented market. Despite the phenomenal success of the private-sector banks in India, the central government chooses to hold on to 27 public-sector banks as standalone entities (many of which are also listed) rather than merging them or selling them to the private sector or to other strategic investors. This is a big impediment to the consolidation and productive development of the Indian banking system.

Japanese banks have been very severely affected by the global financial crisis and the subsequent Japanese recession, which is the country's worst since the Second World War. Large Japanese banks have reported billions in losses and write-downs to the first quarter of 2009. These banks have not been affected by the sub-prime crisis in the US but by the steep fall in Japanese stock prices. This is a homegrown problem, linked to how the Japanese system is set up. Japanese banks take equity stakes in the companies they lend to and, as a consequence, their portfolios are more heavily weighted with equities than any other major banking system. Given that Japanese indices have fallen by more than one-third in a one-year period, the losses are enormous, producing an impact as large as the sub-prime impact on US banks. Added to that is the Japanese recession that is driving up delinquent accounts and additional consumer write-offs. Going by the track record of Japanese regulators and the Japanese system, however, this problem too will be patched over and the banks will be allowed to continue business as usual until another crisis hits.

Banking in Korea too is undergoing a great deal of change, and, according to statements from the Korean government, the state-owned Korea Development Bank (KDB) will be transformed into a holding company by 2010, with its sale to be completed by 2012. This apparently is an objective before President Lee Myung-bak leaves office. The KDB privatization should trigger mergers and acquisitions among financial companies and bring changes in the industry, providing a platform for global expansion and the entry of new businesses.

Chapter 6

The Economics and Politics of Energy

The Asian story can be understood in terms of the mega-trends that are unfolding, the companies that are being spawned to benefit from them, and the tremendous effect this is having around the world. But all that growth and the promise of more to come is really hinged on one great premise: that Asia will have access to all the energy it needs at a cost that it can afford for the next three to four decades, and that it can navigate the plethora of public opinion at home and abroad as it goes about securing its energy resources. While China has become the world's largest producer of automobiles, this leaves the country more dependent on oil imports. Where once it was a net exporter of oil, it currently imports 47 percent of its oil requirements and that figure is expected to rise to 76 percent by 2020. It is no wonder that the Chinese government has become paranoid about building enough oil reserves and grabbing any asset it can find anywhere in the

world and at any price. Unfortunately, the spotlight on Asia's quest
for energy has come at a time when the world is reminded every day
of its obligation to the environment. China and India now rival the
United States and Russia as the top global polluters. Their stance—
that they need to develop their economies before they respond to
environmental concerns—is increasingly unpalatable at home, where
the direct costs of environmental degradation are clearly visible, especially in China.

Access to energy has become both a political and an economic
phenomenon given the varied efforts of the big Asian economies to
secure energy supplies, wherever they can be had. The race for deep
offshore assets and the acquisition of the few available onshore assets
at almost any price has become the name of the game. Chinese petroleum companies are making the greatest impact. The acquisition of
Addax Petroleum (formerly listed on the Toronto Stock Exchange)
at twice the market price, and PetroChina spending billions of dollars in acquiring oil sands in Alberta, Canada, are examples of how
Asian cash is driving energy investments around the world. China has
been aggressive in securing oil supplies, as its timely investments in two
Russian debt-burdened energy giants, Rosneft and Gazprom, show.
The Chinese are obviously not interested in merely bailing out these
two mismanaged companies but in diversifying supply lines by building natural-gas pipelines through northern China.

Currently, the average per-capita consumption of fuel in Europe
and North America is 32 times that in China. Even a cursory look at
the energy-consumption patterns and lifestyle choices that Asians are
making shows that these emerging nations will need far more resources
then they actually possess or are able to acquire at present. China's
oil imports have increased by 32 percent every year for the past 25
years (though it began from a very low base), while India's increased
by 10 percent annually over that same period. China and India are
the second- and third-largest importers of crude oil today, with
3.5 million and 2.5 million barrels per day (bpd), respectively. These
imports reflect nearly half of China's total daily consumption of 7.3
million barrels and over 75 percent of India's daily consumption
of 3.2 million barrels. Japan, at 3.9 million bpd, remains the largest
Asian importer though Japanese imports have actually declined over a

20-year period, as have Korea's. Asia as a whole imports two-thirds of its total crude-oil requirements.

While consumption has been growing exponentially in the Asia-Pacific region, it is also the region that has seen absolutely no increase in crude reserves over the past 25 years, which has remained stagnant at 34 billion barrels. Globally, reserves have increased from over 600 billion barrels to over 1.3 trillion barrels in that time. Outside of the Middle East, the biggest increases in reserves have occurred in Venezuela, which now accounts for 80 percent of the total reserves in Central and South America, and in Nigeria, Libya, Sudan, Gabon, and the Congo, which account for 80 percent of all known reserves in Africa.

Africa is now front and center in the race to secure stable longer-term supplies of energy and mineral resources by the world's leading developed and emerging nations alike. Africa today supplies more oil to the US (essentially from Nigeria) and China than the Middle East does. China has begun to improve its relationships with Africa, including with regimes that may not be palatable to Western governments and large oil companies. China's controversial investments in Africa include US$1 billion in Angola; US$5 billion in Niger; a deep and ongoing energy relationship with Sudan; and potentially large investments in the Democratic Republic of Congo. Also controversial is its relationship with Iran and the energy joint ventures it has pursued with the National Iranian Oil Company. Malaysia too has decided to hedge its future energy needs with a stronger relationship with the Iranians and there have been several projects announced between the two. India, for its part, has been investing in Nigeria in both upstream (oil and gas fields) and downstream (refineries and LNG [liquified natural gas] terminals) projects, from which it expects to source around 5 percent of its requirements. It has also been investing in fields in Russia and Vietnam.

The aggressive and desperate search for stable energy sources could also become a source of tension between nations. Japan has been a long-time investor in Western Australia and has been the largest purchaser of natural resources, especially gas. Gas supplies from Western Australia are critical to provide power for its export industries and Japanese banks have traditionally financed projects here. The North West Shelf Venture, one of the world's largest gas development projects, for example, was financed by the Japanese Exim Bank in 1989 and today supplies 16 percent of Japan's LNG needs. In the recent past Indonesia was the principal supplier of natural gas to Japan but its declining productivity and depleted reserves meant that it has been superseded by Western Australia. Now, however, China has appeared on the scene, with its cash-rich, state-owned companies pushing to accumulate a sizeable stake in Western Australian gas fields and mines, much to the chagrin of Japan.

The emergence over the past two decades of giant state-owned or -influenced energy companies such as PetroChina (the second-largest oil and gas company by net income), Sinopec, and CNOOC from China; ONGC from India; Korea's National Oil Co. (unlisted); and PTT Exploration & Production from Thailand has coincided with growing control over oil reserves and production in the hands of autocratic governments in Africa and Latin America and their nationalized oil companies. The sentiment in oil-exporting countries is that they want control over their resources and prefer doing deals with emerging oil giants from Asia rather than with Western companies. The manner in which Asian companies are conducting business is having a huge impact on the energy world, on energy investments, on the way the West perceives its own energy security, and on the role Western oil giants (known as super-majors) now play in the global energy sweepstakes. Asian oil companies have a higher degree of tolerance for political risk because there is a constant engagement at political and senior government levels between fast-growing Asian economies and countries with which the Western world finds it hard to do business. This willingness to do business in the less-palatable parts of the world is just one of the twists that Asian companies are bringing to the table. The other is the willingness, especially on the part of Chinese companies, to pay well above market prices for assets that they covet. With potential demand far outstripping potential supply and with the cost of producing a barrel of oil outside of the Middle East escalating, it is quite probable that Asian energy companies prefer to pay what seem like ludicrous amounts now rather than scramble around for resources and pay an even higher price later on.

Addax Petroleum Corp., formerly listed in both London and Toronto, built a business model precisely on the premise that Asian state-owned oil companies would be perennial purchasers of properties in places that others may shun. This company actively sought properties in West Africa (Nigeria and Gabon) and in the Kurdistan region of Iraq, hardly the most engaging of places. Nigeria is racked by insurgencies and violence, and Gabon has been ruled by the same kleptocratic political dynasty for more than 40 years. The bulk of the company's production of 135,000 barrels per day comes from Nigeria. By late 2009 the company's management was proved right when China Petroleum and Chemical Corporation (also known as Sinopec) purchased all outstanding stock in the company, paying nearly twice the market price. Just prior to the Addax deal, Sinopec acquired another Canadian-listed entity, Tanganyika Oil Company, with exploration assets in Syria and Tanzania, and paid nearly 19 times revenues and 40 times EBITDA. This valuation was completely out of sync with other deals between junior North American companies with larger revenues and profits than Tanganyika, where the average valuation was five times EBITDA and three times revenues.

The Koreans are no less aggressive. The Korea National Oil Company has made roughly US$20 billion-worth of acquisitions in oil and gas fields in Uzbekistan, Kurdistan, Russia, Peru, and, most recently, in the Gulf of Mexico and Canada, where it purchased Harvest Energy Trust for US$1.8 billion plus the assumption of US$2.3 billion debt. The Korean and Indian oil majors are keenly aware that they are being edged out by China's oil companies but they are not alone.

Large Western oil companies too may well lose out in the long run on emerging oilfields in Africa and South and Central America as energy cooperation among developing nations increases. The bulk of the new oil exploration and production efforts are being undertaken in deep offshore locations or in redeveloping existing fields that were damaged or mismanaged by national oil companies through overproduction or outdated technology. Though they may possess the necessary capital, the Asian oil companies lack the state-of-the-art technology needed to undertake exploration activities on their own. Global oil companies such as BP, Chevron, Royal Dutch Shell, and Exxon Mobil therefore have an opportunity to add to their reserves by acting as operators or minority partners in giant long-gestation fields. Similarly, the opportunity for oil-services companies remains undiminished. Surprisingly, a big beneficiary of the oil exploration and development drive across the globe are oilfield services companies such as Schlumberger, Halliburton, Weatherford, and Baker Hughes. For example, when Rosneft, the Russian oil-and-gas exploration company, obtained exploration rights in North Africa, it lacked the local expertise to explore gas fields and turned to Schlumberger to deliver on marshalling local resources and for its understanding of the operating conditions.

Asian companies have taken up the challenge of deep-sea exploration, which is expected to remain funded despite the overall slump in prices and cutbacks in production. Indian offshore-drilling-and-services company Aban Offshore Ltd. is a good example of a local drilling company that has a number of competitive strengths and a very strong operating track record (23 years and US$1.4 billion in revenues). While it cannot compare in scope and size with the likes of Transocean or Dolphin Offshore, its acquisitions in Europe will help bridge the gap. When China Oilfield Services Ltd. (COSL), one of the larger Asian companies (with revenues of US$1.7 billion), purchased Norway's Awilco Offshore, the acquisition added US$200 million to COSL and, more importantly, gave it the assets of the world's eighth-largest oil-drilling company. Singapore-based Sembcorp Marine, which manufactures drilling rigs, is also a well-regarded player.

In Gas We Trust

Gas consumption from all sources, including coal-bed methane (CBD) and unconventional gas, is expected to see strong growth in the Asia-Pacific region. According to the US Department of Energy, India and China's respective consumption of natural gas is still very low, at just 8 percent and 3 percent of their respective energy mixes. Between now and 2030, however, the expectation is that China's consumption will rise by 5 percent and India's by 4 percent. Figure 6.1 shows the increase in global consumption of natural gas over the 50-year period from 1980–2030. Emerging Asia currently accounts for 9 percent of global gas consumption, which is expected to increase to 25 percent by 2030. China and India will together almost triple their current annual consumption, to 11 trillion cubic feet, while the rest of emerging Asia will increase consumption from six trillion to 14 trillion cubic feet over this time.

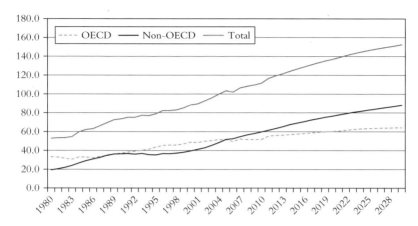

Figure 6.1 Global natural-gas consumption (trillion cubic feet), 1980–2030
SOURCE: EIA

The current and future demand for gas for a variety of industrial and transportation uses, including powering commuter buses and taxi-cabs, as well as for cooking fuel and power generation, augurs well for suppliers and the distribution and logistics companies involved. Despite massive discoveries of natural gas all over the Asia-Pacific region that will more than double domestic output, there is still a considerable gap that needs to be filled with imports for most of emerging Asia, Japan, Korea, and Taiwan. Massive projects in Australia, Indonesia, and Qatar will drive supplies and keep prices low. In Australia alone projects worth nearly US$200 billion have been identified. Australia has over 200 tril-lion cubic feet of reserves and if most of these projects come on stream it will bring in over-supply and lower prices for a long time, benefiting the likes of Japan, Taiwan, and China, where demand will continue to rise. This will drive higher retail prices but keep purchase prices lower.

The key to getting much-needed natural-gas supplies to Asia is there-fore the infrastructure to transport the gas from production sites to final users. Politics has so far trumped common sense in the creation of trans-national gas pipelines from production centers in the Caspian or Iran to other parts of Asia. The only other way of connecting big markets such as China and India to prolific producing regions is through ocean trans-portation, which would necessitate the use of giant cryogenic tankers, liquification plants, and LNG terminals/re-gasification plants, all of which would be prohibitively expensive. Qatar Gas Transport Company and other shipping lines such as Malaysian Shipping and Teekay LNG are among the largest LNG transporters who will benefit from Asia's growing demand for natural gas. Qatar has an edge over others given its dominant position in LNG production and the fact that it has the world's largest gas reserves (900 trillion cubic feet). It is in the process of building the world's largest fleet of LNG tankers (thus betting that many of the overland cross-border pipelines being contemplated may never materialize or be significantly delayed); at the end of 2008 it had 29 ships and, based on orders placed with Korean shipyards, this will increase to 58 by 2010. There are around 220 LNG tankers in use today, the bulk of which have been built by Korean shipbuilders Samsung Heavy Industries, and Daewoo Shipbuilding and Marine Engineering Company. Of the 150 new ships on order worldwide, 100 are to be built by Korean shipyards; at an average cost of US$250 million apiece, this will contribute significantly to their revenues. In 2009, Samsung Heavy charged Qatar Gas a record price of US$286 million for each of four new ships (the largest ever built for the LNG industry at 266,000 cubic meters). Samsung Heavy and Daewoo Shipbuilding between them have a backlog of 80 LNG tankers for various LNG carriers.

The gas shipped using LNG tankers is delivered to purpose-built terminals that then re-gasify the liquid natural gas. Petronet LNG is the most important company in India's natural-gas procurement and distribution industry. The company is a joint venture between some of the largest Indian oil and gas companies, including GAIL and ONGC Ltd., and French energy company Gaz de France. The economics of Petronet's business is linked to gas prices and to that extent there is a bit of earnings volatility. But the company is also a play on the volume of gas demand in India, which has been growing exponentially. Given this scenario, Petronet has doubled the gas-handling capacity at its plant in Dahej, Gujarat. Revenues have compounded by 35 percent over a five-year period to 2009.

Domestic gas pipelines are a lucrative business, especially as supplies are now more reliable and the number of downstream users is growing. Perusahaan Gas Negara (PGN), with 2009 revenues of US$1.3 billion, is one of Indonesia's largest gas transporters and distributors. GAIL India Ltd. (2009 revenues of US$5.2 billion) is a near-monopoly gas pipeline operator in India. The company operates 8,000 km of pipelines but realizes that it needs to accelerate investments to expand the pipeline network and wants to invest US$10.5 billion to double its capacity. The problem is that the company, though publicly listed, is controlled by the government and requires layers of approvals before it can actually proceed. Not surprisingly, then, despite having a superior financial track record and vastly superior profitability and capital efficiency, the company trades at a discount to much smaller and less-profitable domestic competitors such as Gujarat Gas Ltd., which owns a network of pipelines but focuses on supplying compressed natural gas to the transportation industry. This company and Indraprastha Gas Ltd., another small piped-gas supplier to major metropolitan areas, are very profitable enterprises that consistently report a high return on capital.

Hong Kong and China Gas, one of the oldest utilities in Asia, is tapping into the growing demand in Hong Kong for cleaner fuels. It supplies 85 percent of Hong Kong's energy needs and is making significant investments in LPG facilities across Hong Kong and in 30 cities in mainland China. XinAo Gas is a gas distribution company in China. In two decades it has become the largest distributor outside of the big four Chinese companies (PetroChina, Sinopec, CNPC, and CNOOC), supplying piped gas to households and businesses in 60 cities (including Beijing) and supplying LPG cylinders and compressed natural gas through 70 filling stations. It is the only company outside of the big four to have obtained a license from the Chinese government to directly import the natural gas it needs for its operations.

Refining

If bio-fuel advocates have their way, there may not be any need to establish new petroleum-refining capacities because all incremental fuel supply will come from ethanol. But that is not the case. There is a solid growth expectation for the growing consumption of petroleum products for the next decade or more, which is driving the expansion of refinery capacity. The expectation is that demand for refined products in the Asia-Pacific region will grow by close to a million bpd each year until 2020, of which China's demand growth accounts for half. In the mid-1990s, there was a rush to set up refining capacity in the Asia-Pacific region in anticipation of strong regional growth. However, the Asian financial crisis and the subsequent economic slump effectively meant that there was refining overcapacity well into the next decade. However, economic growth over the past 10 years has meant that there could be a refining shortage in Asia over time. The International Energy Agency (IEA) estimates that oil consumption will grow by 3.3 percent a year in Europe, while in the US it will grow by 0.26 percent.

Chinese and Indian refiners are emerging as the growth engines in the crude-oil refining capacities, with Reliance Industries in particular crafting a very consistent strategy to become a dominant player in global energy supply. Reliance Industries has become the owner of the world's largest standalone refinery complex, with 1.24 million barrels per day (mbpd) at a single location (to make a comparison, BP Plc has 2.7 mbpd spread over 17 refineries). Despite there being very significant capacity additions under way in India, pricing distortions between the domestic and international market will result in most of the output from the new capacities going to the export market. Price distortions occur because of the subsidies paid to refiners supplying to the domestic market in light of the sensitive nature of fuel prices, which hamper refiners' cash flow and profitability since subsidy payments are inevitably delayed. Price controls on refined fuels are also the norm for other Asian refining markets including China, where the government sets retail prices. The only saving grace is that the export capacities are huge and will result in India becoming a net exporter of refined products, mainly to China but also to Europe and the US, where no new refineries have been built since 1976. The IEA has also forecast that North American refiners will leave 25 percent of capacity idle by 2014.

China too has severe pricing distortions, but all current and future capacity expansions will be focused on the domestic market, leaving refineries in India and the Middle East to cater to the developed world.

S-Oil Corp., a major South Korean refiner and petrochemical producer, has commenced building one of that country's largest refineries, with a capacity of 300,000 bpd. S-Oil is a diversified downstream company that operates three businesses; petroleum products, petrochemicals, and lube-oil base stock, a product that it launched in South Korea nearly 40 years ago. Similarly, Petron is the dominant refinery in the Philippines, producing 180,000 bpd of refined products, 40 percent of the country's total. However, given recent overcapacity and a large capital buildup, most of these refineries are suffering from poor returns on capital.

Capacities in Asia, and India in particular, are coming up at a time of tremendous environmental concern and the need to produce lighter products that comply with new clean-fuel standards. The newer refineries are geared to do just that, using the latest technologies and at considerably lower cost, giving them an edge in a very competitive space. However, given the quantifiable expected demand growth over the next decade it is very likely that there will be a demand/supply imbalance in favor of the refiners. A total increase in refining capacity of between 7.5 million bpd and 9.5 million bpd is expected by the middle of the next decade and will be largely concentrated in the Middle East, India and China. It is expected that despite all the capacity additions there will be a 5.6 million bpd refining shortage by 2020. This should lead to favorable refining margins for the foreseeable future. This may be an optimistic scenario since there is also a simultaneous effort to increase the bio-fuel capacity. However, the refining industry experience is such that more projects are announced than are actually completed or even begun, for that matter. While India has a number of domestic and foreign refining companies competing for market share, China has a virtual duopoly, with PetroChina and Sinopec holding the bulk of market share.

Power to the People

Power consumption is growing across the continent, but China is the world's largest producer and second-largest consumer of energy. According to some estimates, for China to achieve its 2020 GDP growth goals of quadrupling its per-capita GDP over 2000 levels, it will need to increase its energy capacity by 120 percent from current levels of 450,000MW. China will continue to be one of the world's largest markets for power generation for a long time to come and the pace at which it puts up power projects is unrivalled. In 2007, for example, it put up 90,000MW of power capacity.

China has not lost sight of the unbeatable economics of a large production base of conventional coal-fired plants. The country was dotted with small, inefficient coal-fired plants with a generating capacity of less than 100MW, but most of these have been replaced with plants with a minimum generation capacity of 500MW. While this may exasperate environmentalists, it is practical from China's point of view. Power is needed and the cheaper the better: it is hard to beat the cost of coal-fired plants given their energy input/output ratio and the fact that China has the world's largest coal reserves. China's heavy manufacturing industries are power-intensive, and power cost forms a key component of their total cost.

However, as China seeks to reduce its energy intensity by 20 percent by 2020, this fuel mix will have to change. Currently, 72 percent of its energy comes through coal, followed by hydro at 23 percent, with nuclear fuel at around 1 percent. China's drive for efficiency in electricity generation and use provides an opportunity for utilities and generators outside of China to bid for generation assets. The Korean power company Korea Electric Power, for example, has said it will acquire 14 power plants in China's Shanxi province for US$158.5 million through a joint venture. China's steel industry, which consumes nearly one-fifth of all electricity generated, is being restructured and the government has shut down almost 50 million tons of capacity that did not or could not meet new energy-efficiency standards.

India, for its part, has begun to remedy severe shortages in its generation capacity, where peak shortages consistently hit 12 percent or more. Currently, it has a total capacity of 150,000MW and a per-capita consumption of around 600Kwh (the North American average is 10,000Kwh per annum, while in China it is 2,500Kwh). The government's objective is to raise generating capacity to a minimum of 230,000MW by 2017.

Though China has the largest coal reserves in the world and India has the fourth-largest, it is Indonesian coal miners that will benefit most from the rapid expansion of coal-fired power plants in China and India. Indonesian coal is of better quality since it has very low ash content, and demand is expected to grow at 2 percent a year for the next several years. Bumi Resources, in particular, is in a position to be an even bigger player and currently plans on doubling its current annual output to 100 million tons by 2012. It currently controls 22 percent of Indonesian coal production and, not surprisingly, the Chinese have already started looking at ways to establish a longer-term relationship with the company. Its expansion plans are being funded with a loan from the Chinese government. Keeping in mind the fact that Indonesia too is expanding its coal-fired generation capacities, the Indonesians are likely to restrict exports, which will drive up the price of coal at a faster pace, to the benefit of coal exporters.

While China may be a larger market, India offers a larger choice of companies—equipment manufacturers, generators, and distributors—directly involved with the power and energy infrastructure. Chinese power companies are tightly controlled by the state and only a few have actually listed. Some smaller equipment manufacturers are available to the investing public but other than generating-companies such as China Yangtze Power, which generates power from the Three Gorges Dam, and Datang International Power Generation Company, there are few names that can provide exposure to China's massive power sector. In addition to a broad spectrum of power stocks in India, also available to global investors are listed Indian subsidiaries of global MNCs. These include Siemens India (with revenues of US$2 billion), ABB India (US$1.6 billion), and Areva T&D India (US$600 million).

Bharat Heavy Electricals Ltd. (BHEL) is the largest power-equipment manufacturer in India. The company has over the past half-century installed 90,000MW of thermal generation capacity (mostly coal-fired) across India. It produces more than 180 products, including transformers, and offers turnkey solutions to the power sector in India and to a number of Asian countries. The company will be doubling its annual manufacturing and installation capacity to 20,000MW by 2012.

Larsen & Toubro is one of India's largest energy infrastructure companies. It competes with BHEL in providing complete turnkey solutions to the power sector. It builds both gas- and coal-fired plants and has built more than 100 plants. The company also provides equipment for India's nuclear-energy plants. KEC International puts up power plants and is involved with railway electrification projects. Reliance Infrastructure may be a relative newcomer but is one of the top players in India's energy infrastructure. The company has a tie-up with the Shanghai Electric Corp. to make boilers, turbines, and generators. Indian power-generating firms have placed orders for equipment to generate 26,000MW with Chinese firms such as Shanghai Electric Group Co. Ltd., Dongfang Electric Corp., and Harbin Power Equipment Co. Ltd.

Dongfang Electric Corp. has US$4 billion in revenues and a suite of power-generation products for thermal, hydro, wind, and nuclear power plants. While thermal power is the largest component of its business, the company has made a big bet on wind energy and wind turbines have been a fast-growing segment for the company.

China, India, and the United States are all reportedly very keen on developing coal-liquification technology that converts coal into fuel oil or synthetic oil. Sasol, the largest oil company in South Africa, another coal-rich nation, has successfully implemented a coal refinery that produces this synthetic oil.

Great Eastern Energy Corp. (GEEC) was the first Indian company to list on the Alternative Investment Market (AIM) in London and is the first to commercialize production of coal-bed methane gas (CBM) in India. CBM is one of the cleanest-burning fuels, with almost zero emissions. The stock has provided an annualized return of 37 percent since it listed on the AIM in 2005, even though it has only just begun gas production. The company has completed 58 wells, is currently drilling another 150, and has put in place a network of pipelines to move gas from its fields to industrial users. It has estimated reserves at 1.9 trillion cubic feet and has secured deals to supply 12 million cubic feet of gas per day from gas fields that are conveniently located in the steel-producing region. GEEC has partnered with US oil-services major Halliburton Co. to use the latest fracturing techniques for extraction.

Another AIM-listed CBM producer is Green Dragon Gas Ltd., which operates in China and has reserves of roughly 25 trillion cubic feet of gas. Like Great Eastern Energy, this company has a first-mover advantage in a gigantic market. As the first CBM company in China it had first choice of locations and selected five sites located close to transportation infrastructure and industrial end-users. It added a sixth gas field through an acquisition. It has so far drilled close to 200 wells.

Companies that produce CBM successfully should be more valuable than conventional gas companies because these projects are riskier in the initial stages and of much longer gestation. So companies that actually move into commercial production will carry a lot of value.

BP Plc, one of the largest CBM producers in the world, is betting big on producing the gas in Indonesia, which, like India and China, is ideally suited for producing CBM. Indonesia is estimated to have reserves of 450 trillion cubic feet, though commercial production has yet to begin. A BP Plc-led consortium has signed a production-sharing agreement with the Indonesian government to develop a field with 4 trillion cubic feet of reserves. This could be a prelude to opening up another front in the global effort to develop clean sources of fuel. The larger Chinese, Indian, and Indonesian energy companies are also actively seeking out CBM concessions; PetroChina and Indonesia's national energy company, Ephindo, have already signed production-sharing contracts with their respective governments.

Both India and China are focusing on developing their transmission grids while racing to establish new capacities. China has two giant power-grid companies—the State Grid Corp. and the China Southern Power Grid, with revenues of US$164 billion and US$41 billion respectively, making them the largest distribution companies in the world. Both are unlisted state-owned enterprises, though given their massive expansion plans they may have to turn to the public markets for financing at some point. The Power Grid Corporation of India (US$15 billion in revenues), on the other hand, is India's national operator and is a listed entity. Power Grid Corp. has increased its profitability over several years, growing its RoE from 10 percent in 2003 to 14 percent at present.

The nuclear option, while not a cheap source of power, is preferred by many nations because of its lack of emissions. Energy-starved South Korea, which has not been aggressive in securing its future energy needs, is taking the nuclear route in a big way. Eight of the 50 nuclear reactors being built in the world today are in South Korea. Japan Steel Works (JSW) Ltd. is a specialized producer of atomic-reactor equipment and manufactures for leading nuclear-engineering companies. The company is expanding its current capacity to produce equipment for five nuclear reactors a year to 12. Areva is one of JSW's major clients and has won orders in China worth over US$7 billion.

China is also working to develop nuclear-equipment manufacturing capability and the US-based Westinghouse Electric (77 percent owned by Toshiba of Japan) has been instrumental in working with the Chinese government and companies in transferring know-how and jointly working on new designs. Shanghai Electric and Harbin Power Equipment have been winning orders for portions of the reactor equipment (pressure vessels and steam generators), and this segment can grow into a sizeable portion of its business.

After it secured the nuclear cooperation agreement with the US, India has become a very significant player in the nuclear-power scene and has very aggressive plans to set up nuclear-power plants. At present, just 3 percent of Indian power generation comes from nuclear energy. After China, which is setting up 125 reactors, and Russia, which is setting up 44, India is the third-largest player, with 38 reactors in the works, which will expand its nuclear capacity from 4,100MW at present to 63,000MW by 2032. India will implement the bulk of its nuclear plans through the government-controlled and unlisted Nuclear Power Corporation (NPC), denying investors an opportunity to get in the game early.

The India–US nuclear deal could end up benefiting US firms such as GE, Westinghouse Electric, and Babcock & Wilcox. In late July 2009, two sites in India on which US energy companies could possibly build reactors were announced. India has announced plans to build two 10,000MW reactors for which US companies could bid. French nuclear-energy giant Areva SA has already announced plans involving strategic alliances with Indian construction and engineering firms to build two reactors on India's west coast and sites have been set aside for Russian reactors as well. France and Russia could turn out to be big beneficiaries of India's proposed US$100 billion investment in nuclear energy.

Hindustan Construction Co. is building a 2,000MW nuclear power plant, Asia's largest, in the Southern Indian state of Tamil Nadu. Areva has proposed to supply two 1,650MW reactors for NPC's projects in Rajasthan and Maharashtra. Indian companies such as Tata Power, Reliance Power, GMR, Lanco, and others have been holding talks with foreign companies, which are not allowed to develop nuclear projects independently unless and until Indian laws are amended. For US companies, in particular, the need for clarity on potential liabilities is critical before they embark on any project. This is less of an issue for French and Russian companies. With these needs in mind, the Indian government is currently working on a legal and regulatory framework that will speed up investments in this sector.

GE Hitachi Nuclear Energy Ltd. and Westinghouse Electric Co. plan to use India as a low-cost supplier of nuclear parts for export to the US and Europe, making use of the country's extensive skills in high-precision manufacturing. In order to keep costs low enough to supply cost-competitive power to India, GE Hitachi has said it plans to localize up to 70 percent of production, while Westinghouse plans to use local manufacturing and labor for up to 80 percent of its work. Once that expertise is transferred, both firms plan to turn to their Indian partners to help meet global demand for nuclear-reactor parts. GE Hitachi has signed cooperation agreements with three Indian companies: Larsen & Toubro Ltd., Bharat Heavy Electricals Ltd., and Bharat Forge Ltd. Westinghouse has signed an agreement with Larsen & Toubro and is negotiating three more.

Tail Winds or Head Winds: The Asian Renewable-Energy Story

While strenuous efforts are being made to set up significant power-generation capacities across nations, the key to reducing the gap between demand and supply is probably held by investment in renewable sources. The race to set up alternative energy supplies in Asia is a reflection of how China and India are pursuing the development of renewable energy. India was one of the first countries to embrace renewable energy, especially wind power, and was the first to establish a government ministry for non-conventional energy sources. Today China and India rank among the top five producers of renewable energy in the world (the others being the US, Spain, and Germany). These five nations have a total share of 77 percent of the world's wind-generating capacity. China (12,000MW) and India (9,600MW) have respectively a 10 percent and 8 percent share of the world's wind-power capacity and around 90 percent of the total wind-energy capacity in Asia (24,000MW). These shares are likely to increase as both nations continue to invest heavily in wind power. It is very likely that the

US, China, and India will be the three main drivers of incremental wind-energy capacity additions in the future. The Chinese government has a target of producing 15 percent of its total energy requirement from wind by 2020. Studies have shown that China has the ability to produce 100,000MW of power from wind.

Suzlon Energy is a remarkable story of Asian enterprise and competitiveness. This Indian company is today the world's foremost supplier and aggregator of wind-power technology, turbines, components, and turnkey solutions.[1] Between 2005 and 2009 revenues grew by 67 percent annually to US$5.7 billion. The company is aggressive and has a global operation that now includes a 90 percent ownership of REpower AG, one of the world's top wind-turbine manufacturers. The company's operations now include research and development in Europe, manufacturing in India and China, and installations worldwide. Now that wind-power generation is no longer an unproven "alternative" but very mainstream, companies like Suzlon should continue to attract attention despite recent financial problems.

The fact that the top five global markets for wind energy and a few others put out around 25,000MW to 30,000MW of capacity each year has created a global market for wind turbines worth US$47 billion a year. China too is creating an entire end-to-end supply chain for wind energy. Companies such as Xinjiang Goldwind Science & Technology Company, China High Speed Transmission Equipment Co., and China Wind Power International Corporation have begun to emerge in this space. Another interesting play on the wind-energy market is American Superconductors, a NASDAQ-listed US company that produces wind-turbine electrical systems and power converters. It has benefited from the surge in installed capacity in China, and its current revenue base of US$400 million is very likely to accelerate in the years ahead. It recently acquired a European wind-turbine design company, which will expand its product offerings.

But generation capacities based on renewable resources can potentially be a double-edged sword, as experience in the hydro-power industry in China, Australia, and Pakistan has shown. In the past five years, severe drought conditions in key hydro-power producing regions have led to a spike in demand for power generated using conventional fossil fuels (mainly diesel). This sharp spike and subsequent sustained growth in demand led to the first major surge in oil prices to above US$50 a barrel (bbl) in 2005–06, which eventually resulted in heightened speculation and a jump in price to US$147/bbl.

China's reliance on hydro power is a key risk since it has been government policy to encourage small hydro projects across the country. It now has 50 percent of the world's total small hydro capacity and there are still more projects under way. There could be serious fallout in the oil industry from the huge investments being made in hydro power that may not be able to fulfill its potential and thus force a very large shift to conventional fuel sources.

Today's reality is that Asia is underpowered, especially when considering the concentration of humanity in China and India. Asian demand for energy is rising at a time when the potential of renewable energy is the center of attention for industry, consumers, and policy makers alike; and Asia is the ideal market to unroll it since the existing power infrastructure is limited. It is no surprise, therefore, that Asian economies are emerging among the leading investors in various forms of renewable technology.

Veolia Environment has an energy division that offers a waste-to-energy technology that treats waste as a renewable resource. According to the company, 140 million tons of it is burned in waste-to-energy plants worldwide, which is equivalent to using 220 million tons of crude. The technology provided by this company is of tremendous use to the rapidly developing countries in Asia.

Geothermal fields in the Philippines have been systematically developed by PNOC Energy Development Corporation (EDC), which was owned by the government but is now listed on the Manila Stock Exchange. The company, which produces around 1,400MW of energy from six geothermal steam fields, is now the second-largest geothermal power producer in the world and controls 60 percent of the Philippines' geothermal capacity. The company is part of the Philippine National Oil Corporation group that is also the country's largest producer of crude oil and petrochemicals. Among the renewable-fuel sources being looked at by the group is a 30MW power plant fired with the waste generated after the crushing of sugarcane.

Energy Efficiency: A Major Theme in Asia?

While the Chinese government has succeeded in reducing the energy consumption per ton of output in its manufacturing sector (especially in its large and diverse steel industry), this has to be balanced against the phenomenal growth expected in personal automobile usage—from today's 30 million vehicles to 225 million vehicles in 2030. The number of automobiles in India, too, is expected to accelerate quickly from its current base of 15 million with the introduction of low-cost models. Typically, smaller, fuel-efficient cars have driven all the volume growth in the Indian and Chinese markets. In India, the Tata Nano has been designed and tested to deliver 56 miles per gallon or 20 kilometers per liter. These standards are well above the tough new fuel-efficiency standards prescribed for US auto makers (35.5 miles per gallon/15.44 kilometers per liter). While proliferation of the personal automobile in emerging countries continues to keep the pressure on fuel prices it can be reasonably expected that auto technology will also continue to evolve. Just over a decade ago 18 mpg was the US standard for automobiles manufactured in the US. This was subsequently raised to 27 mpg or 13 km per liter, which was raised further in 2009.

Where the Indian private sector has taken the lead, various local governments in China too are actively encouraging the development of fuel-efficient technologies. SAIC Motor Corp., for example, the largest Chinese auto maker (which is listed as an A-share in Shanghai), is being backed by the local Shanghai city government (the company's part owner) in developing hybrid technology, and the city's civil service is being actively solicited by the government to opt for hybrid cars. SAIC released a hybrid car called the LaCrosse into the Chinese market in 2008. The company has also made very clear progress with an electric car and another hybrid model which will be released in 2010, as well as working to adapt fuel-cell technology developed by GM. The city government is also offering all purchasers of what it calls "new-technology vehicles" a 20 percent rebate on the purchase price of the car in 2010 and 2011. The municipality is also installing battery-charging infrastructure in the city for electric cars and has said that it will introduce road tax breaks for these and other new-technology cars. Twelve other Chinese municipalities are offering similar incentives for auto makers to produce fuel-efficient vehicles and directly subsidize consumer purchases.

Like in everything else they do, the Chinese are clear in their objective to be the world's largest and cheapest producer of fuel-efficient and environmentally friendly vehicles. This is one reason to be optimistic about electric-automobile manufacturers such as BYD Co. and Indian mini-car makers such as Tata Motors.

Endnote

1. For a fuller account, see my book *India: An Investor's Guide to the Next Economic Superpower*, John Wiley & Sons, 2006.

Chapter 7

Political Stability: Asia's New Investment Catalyst

An unlikely investment catalyst has emerged on the Asian invest-ment scene: political stability. This phenomenon has been unfolding for years and is driving a growing momentum of economic reform and bringing together Asian nations like never before.

A New Phenomenon in Asia

Politics and political stability in Asia has, for the most part, been a constantly shifting sand dune. Unlike the European definition of its political and economic union there is no holistic effort to forge a unique Asian political and economic identity. However, the building block that Asian nations have worked to put in place and encourage in one another through intra-regional forums is one of political stability. For every military coup in Thailand or act of repression in Myanmar there is an elective and representative process taking root elsewhere. However, there is still a significant disparity in the political spectrum in Asia: from tribal monarchies in the Persian Gulf; theocratic democracies such as Iran; emerging democracies such as Indonesia, Cambodia, and the Philippines; totalitarian states such as China; and noisy democracies such as India. In reality, though Asia may be far from being a unified and cohesive political construct like the European Union, it has made rapid strides in evolving stability and political maturity.

Though stable for the most part, political risk is still a key variable is assessing the volatility of returns from Asia, and should remain so. Political stability is a relatively new phenomenon, but it can be taken for granted in many parts of Asia. However, there are also constant reminders of the instability that once was and that can be again if the hard-earned peace and stability dividend is squandered. A politically stable region such as East Asia has within it unstable elements such as Thailand; unstable regions such as the Middle East and South Asia have islands of strong growth and internal stability such as India and Israel and politically cohesive nation-states such as Abu Dhabi. For global investors, the political trends that have evolved in the more dynamic regions of Asia over the past 20 years can be considered to be very favorable and point the way forward for the rest of the continent.

A more stable political environment points to better governance standards since it leads to greater institutionalization of the economy thus improving the quality of the investment canvas. Growing political maturity in Asia and the relative sense of stability that it has brought to several important economies and economic regions has been an indisputable reason for the growing consumer lifestyle and economic acceleration.

Stability and Maturity Vs. Grassroots Democracy

When we talk about political maturity in the Asian context, we are not talking about the evolution of democracy across the region because true and sustainable democracy still evades a number of rapidly developing Asian economies. Rather, what we're talking about is political stability across the region, however flawed the democratic process may

Table 7.1:   Political Instability Index: A cross-section of the 2008 rankings

Country	Index Score*	Risk to Political Stability
Japan	3.8	Low
Oman	3.9	Low
Hong Kong	4.0	Low
United Arab Emirates	4.1	Moderate
Qatar	4.1	Moderate
Vietnam	4.3	Moderate
Taiwan	4.3	Moderate
India	4.5	Moderate
Singapore	4.7	Moderate
China	4.8	Moderate
Kuwait	5.5	Moderate
Bahrain	5.5	Moderate
Saudi Arabia	6.1	High
Indonesia	6.8	High
The Philippines	6.8	High
Bangladesh	7.5	Very High
Pakistan	7.8	Very High

SOURCE: *The Economist*

* A lower index value indicates greater stability

be in several cases. The *Economist* magazine produces an annual political stability ranking of 161 nations (see Table 7.1) and it is interesting to note how non-democratic nations score on political stability vis-à-vis democratic nations.

East Asia in particular has been blessed with peace for nearly two decades. The institutional mechanism provided by forums such as ASEAN and the explosion of trade between Southeast Asia and China, South Korea, and Japan has been the catalyst for what seems to be sustainable peace among these nations. Several East Asian nations have emerged from the raucous and violent politics of the 1980s that saw considerable destabilization in countries like Indonesia, Malaysia, the Philippines, Thailand, and even China. Even the relatively stable democracy of Taiwan had its share of political problems, including single-party rule and martial law until the 1990s, but today is ranked as one of Asia's stronger democracies and, interestingly enough, above India, which has enjoyed more than 60 years of history as a democracy, as compared to 20 years for Taiwan.

The dysfunctional politics of the past was partly to blame for the economic mismanagement that culminated in the financial crisis of 1997. Now, however, political stability has become a great enabler of economic growth and investor confidence, and the economies that have been able to achieve that stability have benefited significantly from economic development. Political stability is the product of a political system characterized by freedom from military coups and takeovers, by continuity and reliability of government policies, stable laws, and, of late, includes an absence of domestic social tensions. For investors in the West it also includes a more transparent decision-making environment at the government level. Essentially, it is all those factors that lend confidence to investors that the environment to which they commit will not be subject to unexpected change.

The increased recognition being given to the role of institutional infrastructure, whether for trade, finance, or regional security, is enabling further investor confidence and economic growth. Southeast Asia in particular has seen the disastrous consequences that instability and the absence of institutional infrastructure can bring. Key elements of the institutionalization process in Asia are the free-trade structures being put into place, the economic liberalization and openness initiated in no small measure by the fiscal crisis in India in 1991, the Asian crisis in 1997, and the accession of China and Taiwan to the WTO in 2001. The Asian crisis of 1997–98 also resulted in greater political maturity that enabled the construction of a more robust economic system better able to withstand economic shocks.

It seems intuitive that political stability, open economic policies, and wide-ranging protections for investors is probably the best combination to sustain Asian investment. China is increasingly veering toward that system. But China has also been held out as an example of political stability simply by virtue of the fact that it has continuity of government policies and national cohesiveness in implementing its economic and political agenda no matter which group of individuals hold the reins of power. Nevertheless, to investors in the West the absence of democracy is a huge disincentive that cannot be balanced by any other gains. No matter how much China develops its economy, builds its brands, or absorbs high technology it will be viewed with suspicion because it is seen as an undemocratic and closed society.

Though India has always been a democracy with a relatively open society and many of the necessary legal protections in place, a powerful bureaucracy and avaricious politicians have, in the past, generated a distrust among investors that has tainted the entire country. Added to political dysfunction and bureaucratic apathy are the various conflicting pulls of its diverse social fabric. But the fact that India has managed to produce significant opportunities shows that the liberalizing economic system is working, and that there are inherent advantages to participating in a functioning democracy.

Only three Asian nations—India, Israel, and Japan—can be counted as having a multi-decade track record of grassroots democracy. Though India has strong democratic institutions it too went through a brief period of civil turmoil, which led to the imposition of emergency rule in 1976, though this was rescinded a year or so later under popular pressure. But even during that testing period for India's democratic underpinnings, the Indian military did not come into confrontation with its civilian masters in order to "restore democracy," as so many military juntas and dictators in South Asia, for example, have done, repeatedly in some cases.

South Korea has shown signs of a maturing democratic system, while Taiwan has shaken off the fractious political legacy which had established a stable political system but one that was inherently undemocratic. For the bulk of its formative years from 1949 until 1986 Taiwan remained a single-party state in which even the bureaucrats were party members. The state chose the companies and sectors it wished to support and built up a strong system of patronage in creating strong industries and a powerful national economy. In a little over 20 years since multi-party democracy was introduced growth continues while democratic institutions take root.

Cambodia too is a great example of the potential that can be uncovered when political stability is introduced into a severely disrupted economic environment. The country had been all but written off by global investors and was only ever mentioned in global media in relation to the civil war that ended in the early 1990s, when the work of reconstructing the political system began under UN guidance. Since then, the signs of a functioning nation are becoming increasingly evident. Since 1993, Cambodia has had four national elections, the latest in 2008. It has had stable governments in each election cycle, with each government completing its five-year term of office. Since the departure of the communist Khmer Rouge in 1999, the country has enjoyed real peace, and reconstruction has commenced. For the last three years the country has seen annual GDP grow by 10 percent (though inflation tends to be high).

The importance of political stability has been both reflected and reinforced by the changing profile of investors choosing to invest their funds in Asian economies. Increasingly, the momentum of investment in Asia is being driven by cross-investments and trade between Asian nations and by large sovereign Asian investors, who have a better understanding of risks. Asian real estate provides a good example. The US and European capital markets, both debt and equity, were the main sources of finance for global real estate, Asia included. With the financial crisis crimping capital markets from 2007 and into 2009, sovereign funds and banks from the Middle East and private funds from the Asia-Pacific region and Australia have begun to pick up the slack, thus pushing Asia's investment opportunity increasingly into Asian hands.

However, social instability is still a killer of investment opportunities, as several Asian nations are finding out. For example, despite its vast wealth Saudi Arabia's future prosperity is held hostage to the violent upheaval between the monarchy and Islamic extremism. By contrast, the UAE is racing ahead with tremendous political capital behind the current emir and his family. Though for the most part the Arab states of the Gulf Cooperation Council seem to have bridged the physical gap between their traditional tribal ways with their oil wealth and gleaming cities, politics in the Middle East is still rooted in feudal tribalism. Democratic notions are few and where practiced (as in Kuwait and Bahrain, where local elections are permitted) are very limited in scope and exclude women.

Asia's growing wealth also presents a key risk to its political stability: studies have shown that as its wealth grows so does the disparity in its distribution. While income and wealth inequality seems to be an almost-global phenomenon, it is in Asia that the impact is greatest. In China and India, for example, while everyone's standard of living has improved, the greater share of that improvement has gone to fewer people, and such disparities can lead to civil unrest. In India, the people expressed themselves decisively in national elections in 2004, voting out the ruling coalition, which had led India during a period of strong growth and relative stability, primarily because of perceived inequity. In China, where there is no electoral system through which people can express their frustrations, there have been many reports of local protests erupting across a number of regions and encompassing a range of economic issues.

Demographics will play an important part in Asia's political destiny, and youth movements will drive political destinies much as they did in Iraq and Syria in the 1950s and '60s, and in Iran and South Korea in the 1970s. The entire Middle East region has a large population of young people (defined as those below the age of 35). The current median age in Jordan, for example, is 23; in Israel it is 28. This population is expected to double in the next 20 years, triggering a social revolution and presenting a great risk to the social and investment fabric in the region. The current instability in Saudi Arabia merely confirms what can happen when governments neglect to invest in their younger population. But, at the same time, Oman and the UAE are making real efforts to channel their young people into productive lives at all levels of the economy, rather than just at the top level of corporations as many Arab nations have historically done. Not surprisingly, these two nations score very well on the political stability index.

The process of privatization—a common theme across Asia—will be a trigger for improving the quality of domestic workforces in the region, as governments begin to get out of business and focus on managing better governance. Integration with the rest of the world, especially the West, is high on the agenda of many nations, especially in the Middle East where Abu Dhabi, in particular, is preparing for the time when its economy and that of the UAE will be very well integrated with that of Europe and the US. A few of the Middle East nations are emerging as keen developers of manufacturing capability within their borders and, as part of this strategy, are actively investing in global corporations. Financial integration is one way in which Asia nations are plugging into each other and the rest of the world. The result of the national elections in India in 2009 too has been a vote for more economic reform, and privatization of state enterprises is a critical element of that reform.

Asian Security: Pacifism as an Economic Mantra

While Asian energy concerns are well understood, what is of more concern is that its energy and political security needs have been translated into a build-up of military might and political-military alliances. So, despite the large strides made in the decade since the Asian crisis, significant political risks remain. Several democracies are fragile, and, despite an enduring peace in many regions, Asia still remains the most militarized of continents. Its defense spending is astronomical and it is home to several of the world's largest and fastest-growing militaries. Despite the feverish attempts that have been made to tackle problems through regional institutional forums, there remain a number of unresolved border disputes: China–Japan, China–Russia, China–India, China–Vietnam, Japan–Russia, and North–South Korea to mention but a few. Then there is the fragile post-civil-war peace in Sri Lanka, the civil war in Pakistan, a brutal dictatorship in Burma, and a despotic regime in North Korea. Add to these the seemingly intractable and lingering mistrust between India and Pakistan, Israel and Iran, and North and South Korea and it is clear that there are a number of potential triggers for further regional conflict that could easily spill over into other parts of Asia. The volatile Palestinian issue and violent extremism in Saudi Arabia merely add to the potential for trouble.

China is feared in the West for its potentially disruptive economic and military power. Asia's defense spending is on the rise and major Asian nations spend an average of 5–10 percent of their GDP on defense. But while Asia houses some high defense spenders it also has one of the world's most powerful economies that spends a minimal amount on its defense needs. Since the end of the Second World War, Japan has spent less than 1 percent of its GDP a year on defense, which has greatly enhanced both its national savings and its ability to invest. But despite this Japan remains a lost opportunity.

As the world's second-largest economy—with leverage provided by powerful technological, industrial and financial muscle, and worldwide development aid—Japan should have been Asia's natural leader. It was Japanese development assistance that provided the basis of sustainable economic development in East Asia in the 1970s and 1980s. During the Asian economic crisis and for a few years after, development assistance to East Asia reached record levels, running to US$8–10 billion a year. But Japan consistently lacked cohesiveness between its economic ambitions and foreign-policy objectives. Its approach to foreign aid, which has been used as an effective tool by the US, the UK, and other nations, has been fragmented and directionless (see Figure 7.1). China and India, on the other hand, have consciously aligned their foreign policies and diplomacy with their economic interests and have become donor nations, realizing the importance of that tool in furthering their interests.

Despite its considerable economic achievements, Japan has never played a leadership role in Asia but, rather, has always looked at itself as being somehow apart from it. One important reason for Japan's inability to lead is that is has always looked to the US for political and economic direction and, in turn, has been the conduit of US policy in Asia. In a sense the US has been the de facto leader of Asia. With Asian nations increasingly asserting themselves and proving capable of

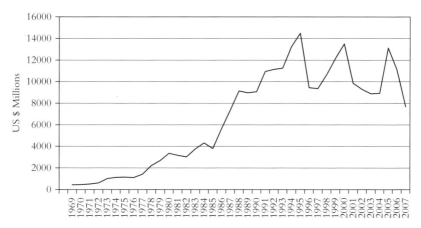

Figure 7.1   Japan's development aid contributions, 1969–2007
SOURCE: OECD–DAC 2009

making their own economic and political choices (for example, Taiwan choosing a political dispensation that clearly advocates closer and conciliatory relations with China), Japan's role, along with it that of the US, has diminished. China has comfortably slipped on the mantle of Asia's next-generation leader.

Despite its economic strides, Japan's political leadership has always been characterized as weak and bereft of strategic vision, which has further weakened and fragmented its pervasive bureaucracy. Such is the nature of Japanese politics that it is impossible to develop coherent policies, especially when it comes to its strategic interests. Moreover, the absence of clear principles that can be projected to the rest of the world and passive reactions to shifting external circumstances are the salient features of Japanese diplomacy since the Second World War. A weak civil society and weak policy think-tanks are also factors that have conspired to keep Japan from assuming the mantle of Asian leadership.

Japanese companies, on the other hand, have proven to be uncanny investors, providing the seed capital to developing Asian economies in the very early stages of their reform process. This was especially true in China and India, long before others came in. Despite that advantage, however, Japan's links with Asia seem to have been set up only to do business in those countries rather than to benefit from trade by importing low-cost goods other than raw material and intermediate inputs into its formidable export machine. It is only after a severe and debilitating recession lasting for more than a decade that Japan is now forging trade links through FTAs with South Korea and some countries in East Asia.

China, like Japan, has the US as its biggest trading partner but has forged very strategic relationships with numerous other trading partners, including Japan, whose export revenues are now linked to its ability to source intermediate goods from China. After a dismal 1990s, Japan began to show some signs of revival in the early part of the millennium but the credit and banking crisis has resulted in a major economic contraction. So intertwined is Japan's industry with the rest of the world, especially the US, and so large is Japan's financial sector that it cannot but suffer harsh consequences as its anemic domestic consumption cannot pick up the slack of lost exports.

The bottom line is that there is a leadership vacuum in Asia, and China is eager and increasingly able to fill it. For any nation to control Asia, it must first control trade and influence events within East Asia. In that sense, though India has been portrayed as a potential Asian leader it has little hope of achieving such a position given the enormous cultural dissimilarities. India is viewed differently by Asian democracies and by states with less-democratic notions. It is a close ally of Israel, and while strong democracies such as Japan and South Korea have been welcoming of India's expanded role in East Asia, countries like China, Indonesia, and Malaysia have been less so. China also has the significant advantage of the huge wealth, knowledge, and the credibility that its Taiwan, Singapore, and Hong Kong connections and the large and enterprising Chinese diaspora in East and Southeast Asia bring to it.

However, despite China's involvement in several border disputes and its tense and sometimes uncooperative relationship with Japan, it remains a great example to other Asian countries of what can be achieved when a nation puts its competitive advantages to good use and focuses on what is possible. What is remarkable is that it is probably the only totalitarian system that has achieved such remarkable and consistent economic progress over decades. Those of us with democratic notions consider it only natural that the absence of democracy, freedom of choice, and that very American notion of the "pursuit of happiness" in totalitarian ideologies such as China's dooms them to eventual failure. While that is usually true, the Chinese have a collective practicality, relentless focus, and immense patience that have enabled an economic system that blends elements of Western capitalism with their home-grown ideologies. This hybrid economic system—a kind of state-directed capitalism—has worked wonders for China and is certainly worth considering as an alternative economic system for other developing economies struggling to balance political freedoms and economic growth.

It is said that people and nations get the leaders and political systems they deserve. In light of the sustained economic development under the current Chinese political system it is reasonable to wonder whether it would perform differently under a different political system. If the Chinese could elect their leaders, would they choose differently? And would those leaders be driven any differently than those currently in power? Would the people behave any differently, save any less, or live less frugally? Would the economy be any more powerful than it is today simply because it is a democracy? Russia may be the closest example we have of a totalitarian system transformed into a market-driven system; apart from the fantastic earnings from energy exports, it has proved to be a dismal political and economic experience for both Russians and their neighbors. Is Russia any better off simultaneously trying to develop its large and diverse economic engine with a fledgling democracy bereft of democratic institutions? The answer is, probably not. The African and West Asian experience in the 1960s and 1970s, where several post-colonial nations tried experimenting with democracy and economic reforms simultaneously, resulted in total failure. The Central Asian experiment of democracy before achieving economic stability has also resulted in demagogic politics cloaked in democratic garments. By comparison, the current Chinese model, which seeks solid economic prosperity before seeking the fruits of political reform, seems to have worked well. It seems to me that China as a democracy would act more or less as it does today.

It is almost counter-intuitive to think of China, rather than Japan, as Asia's natural leader, given the fact that Japan has always acted as a lender of last resort to Asian economies in trouble and played an important and effective role during the 1997–98 crisis. However, in addition to all its other travails, the Japanese financial system and its economy have not fared well during the current downturn and its political leadership has been virtually invisible. There has been a dramatic shrinkage in Japan's automobile and electronics exports, and the country is now running an unprecedented current-account deficit.

That this century will, in all likelihood, be China's may be a hard truth for the likes of Japan and India to swallow—but better they swallow it and emulate China's nimbleness now rather than later, when the race for influence might just degenerate into confrontation.

China: Villain or Hero?

Opinion is divided on whether the US and China will ever engage in a military conflict as the US seeks to protect its hegemony in Asia, and to counter China's growing influence in the race to acquire long-term sources of oil, metals, and minerals, especially in Africa. The current military balance between the two may well be in the favor of the US; however, it has few economic weapons left to undermine China's growing influence. Worries about war over Taiwan may be less of a concern now, especially since Taiwan has realized the significant benefits to be had from an enduring peace with China. For all practical purposes, Taiwan and China are inextricably linked and the links are only getting stronger. Taiwan currently sends 40 percent of its exports to China and the thousands of Taiwanese companies that operate on the mainland have created 10 million jobs there. More importantly from Taiwan's perspective, its companies in China drive almost all of Taiwan's exports there. Taiwan, in turn, is in the process of removing many of the obstacles to Chinese investment on the island. In the first quarter of 2009, the Taiwanese government announced that commercial, industrial, and employee housing in Taiwan is now opened to Chinese investment, as are 101 other sectors. All these steps have been initiated by the Taiwanese government of President Ma Ying-Jeou (a pro-China politician who won a popular mandate in 2008). More importantly, Ma's government is negotiating an Economic Cooperation Framework Agreement (ECFA) with China, prompted by the FTA between China and ASEAN, which excludes Taiwan and could put a lot of pressure on Taiwanese earnings. These are big steps toward permanently eliminating distrust between the two and creating the bedrock for comprehensive trade and investment gains in Taiwan. The two countries have agreed to increase the number of weekly flights between them (from 18 to 54), and several Chinese airlines have already begun to implement the agreement. It is precisely this kind of trade diplomacy that will save the region from conflict. Taiwan is likely to earn a huge peace dividend and will be a disproportionate gainer from a real peace deal with China. Not only will China have an incentive to increase trade with Taiwan, but it will in all likelihood permit an increase in the numbers of tourists to visit Taiwan. The combined impact of these two developments will be significant for Taiwan.

That American influence in much of Asia is declining is evident and that decline is creating a power vacuum. At an ASEAN conference during George W. Bush's first term, more delegates turned up to hear the Chinese premier speak than the US president: the former focused on economic opportunity; the latter on the "war on terror." US influence will continue to decline as long as it remains engaged in wars that continue to erode its political and economic standing in Asia. Just as two world wars in the first half of the last century cemented Britain's decline as an economic and military power, any significant battlefield reverses in the current wars will further damage US credibility, making China's transition to becoming Asia's dominant power that much more credible.

The economic shift described above is most evident in China and India, which will always comprise the bulk of the investment opportunity in Asia. However, a lot of the potential investment opportunity that will unfold in Asia will be influenced by what happens in China. China, above all Asian nations, has the cohesiveness in policy, the sense of purpose, clear growth ambitions, a disciplined and frugal workforce, and a dedicated political leadership to push it along relentlessly to be the leader that Asia now so dearly needs. If China has not yet attained a leadership position in all spheres, whether economic, political, and military, it is just a matter of time. Leadership is not simply about becoming the largest consumer of commodities or resources or the biggest producer of goods and services; rather, it is about real economic and political leadership (not unlike that provided by the United States) that brooks no competitors but fosters alliances and functions as a bulwark for global stability. There is an interesting train of thought that suggests that Mandarin may replace English as the language of global business. This is probably a misplaced sentiment at best. While the world thinks it needs to learn Mandarin in order to work with the Chinese, the Chinese people themselves are desperately trying to learn English. For the Chinese there is no greater symbol that they have arrived than their ability to converse in English, in much the same vein that the previous world economic conquerors, the Japanese, did before them. In a speech in January 2009, Chinese Premier Wen Jiabao said that 300 million Chinese were studying English, preparing for greater integration with the rest of the world. This is a common sentiment expressed by most Chinese, who are aware that much of India's growing economic success is, in part at least, attributable to its grasp of English as well as to its technical prowess.

A number of Chinese business people, bureaucrats, and politicians have been educated in the West, and as a new generation of leaders comes to the fore over the next decade the better will be China's integration with Asia and the world.

China has always been accused of covering its political objectives and economic ambitions behind a veil of secrecy. While there may be opaqueness in the way it speaks of its ambitions, there is clarity and purpose in action. Before any of the developed nations could push through a domestic stimulus package in their legislative branches, China announced a stimulus package worth over half-a-trillion dollars. Speedy political decision-making is the one clear defining difference between China and India. The Chinese government does not have to worry about fickle public opinion, competitive elections, or other democratic distractions. Though it lacks democratic credentials and is yet to be tested as a global leader, there is enough anecdotal evidence to show that China, if it continues to pursue its current track of economic and political expansion, will be the pre-eminent force in the world in the near term. Interestingly enough, democratic processes do exist in China and if a peaceful change of political leadership is one of the criteria for political maturity, then China has it. The peaceful transfer of power happens at all echelons of China's political spectrum and especially with its all-powerful president and prime minister at the end of their terms of office. This is hardly autocratic. A glance at any other totalitarian regime in or outside Asia shows how incumbents cling onto power well after their terms have ended.

The economic and political expansion has triggered suspicions around whether China wants to "rule the world." The fact of the matter is that if China did have such intentions, it would go against the grain, and history would not be on its side. I do not want to sound like an apologist for China but it is more likely that it wants to secure its economic clout and opportunities outside of China while, in turn, becoming a great market for the rest of the world. Part of the fear-mongering has to do with the China Investment Corporation (CIC), also known as the Chinese sovereign fund. With US$200 billion in assets and the possibility of further transfers from Chinese currency reserves, the CIC could potentially become an acquisition vehicle for the Chinese government. But a closer look at its investment strategy and acquisition activities since its inception a few years ago shows that domestic Chinese companies may end up dealing more with it than corporations outside of China. The CIC was created in 2004 and since then a little over 60 percent of its cash has been invested in Chinese state-owned companies, principally in recapitalizing holding companies including those of the Industrial and Commercial Bank of China and the Bank of China, at the direction of the Chinese government.

The CIC's operating model largely mirrors that of any large global pension fund, where resources are allocated to different investment strategies and the execution is managed by third-party managers. Some of its closest relationships are on Wall Street, given that the CIC's managers have a strong global-investment background, and so its early non-Chinese company investments were in privately held firms such as the Blackstone Group and in others such as Morgan Stanley. The Chinese fund has been closely modeled on the Singapore government's US$300 billion sovereign fund. The Chinese fund has tremendous scope for growth, since it represents less than 10 percent of China's currency reserves, and to that extent will continue to play a large role in the global and domestic investment sphere. It is interesting to note that the same level of trepidation is not expressed when sovereign funds from the Middle East pick up stakes in iconic global corporations.

Another source of concern is that China will eventually use its financial muscle and acquisition power to acquire leverage with foreign governments. The negative public reaction in Australia to sustained Chinese investments and takeovers of Australian assets is a microcosm of the kind of resentment that awaits China as it continues to make strategic raw material and energy acquisitions around the world. Many influential investment thinkers also feel that China itself is a potentially volatile place given that tens of thousands of protests are breaking out regularly across the country over social, economic, and political issues. The common view seems to be that there may be some form of violent upheaval in China that could, over time, lead to instability in the world. That upheaval could also lead to some form of democratic process that may make China easier to understand and less complicated to deal with.

Those who think that they may have less to fear from a democratic China may need to re-think that premise, because Chinese objectives and subsequent actions in the global arena will not change. As with any rising power, growing economic and political clout also come with significant opportunities for investors.

As we have seen, unprecedented levels of economic cooperation between East Asian nations, especially after the 1997 financial crisis, have now spread between East Asia and other major Asian nations such as India and Israel. There has also been an increase in the development of social, economic, and political institutional infrastructure in the post Cold-War era that has fostered greater cooperation and, more importantly, begun to provide a huge peace dividend to the vast majority of Asian nations.

Select Bibliography

Aggarwal,Vinod K. and Koo, Min Gyo (eds.) 2008, *Asia's new institutional architecture: Evolving structures for managing trade, financial, and security relations*: Springer.

Case, William 2002, *Politics in South East Asia: Democracy or less*: Curzon.

Chen, Chunlai (ed.) 2009, *China's integration with the global economy: WTO accession, foreign direct investment and international trade*: Edward Elgar.

Chen, Shaohua and Ravallion, Martin 2008, "The Developing World is Poorer than we thought but no less successful in the fight against poverty": World Bank Policy Research Working Paper 4703.

Denoon, David B. H. 2007, *The economic and strategic rise of China and India: Asian realignments after the 1997 financial crisis*: Palgrave Macmillan.

Department of Foreign Affairs and Trade, Australia, 2001, "Subsistence to Supermarket II: Agrifood globalization and Asia."

Ford, Ben 2007, "Challenge for Asia in infrastructure needs," Country Risk, Export Finance and Insurance Corporation, Australia.

Harvard Business Review 2004, *Doing Business in China*: Harvard Business School Pub.

Kidd, John B. and Richter, Frank-Jürgen (eds.) 2005, *Infrastructure and productivity in Asia: Political, financial, physical and intellectual underpinnings*: Palgrave Macmillan.

Lakhera, Mohan L. 2008, *Japanese FDI flows in Asia: Perspectives and challenges*: Palgrave Macmillan.

MacIntyre, Andrew, Pempel, T. J. and Ravenhill, John (eds.) 2008, *Crisis as a catalyst: Asia's dynamic political economy*: Cornell University Press.

Mahbubani, Kishore 2008, *The new Asian hemisphere: The irresistible shift of global power to the East*: PublicAffairs.

Mo, Jongryn and Okimoto, Daniel I. (eds.) 2006, *From crisis to opportunity: Financial globalization and East Asian capitalism*: Washington, DC: Brookings Institution Press.

Palacios, Juan J. (ed.) 2008, *Multinational Corporations and the emerging network economy in Asia and the Pacific*: Routledge.

PricewaterhouseCoopers, "Eye on Asia," *Global Real Estate Now*, June 2008.

Rowen, Henry S., Gong Hancock, Marguerite and Miller, William F. (eds.) 2007, *Making IT: The rise of Asia in high tech*: Stanford University Press.

The McKinsey Quarterly, "The value of China's emerging middle class," 2006 special edition.

Timmermann, Martina and Tsuchiyama, Jitsuo (eds.) 2008, *Institutionalizing northeast Asia: Regional steps towards global governance*, United Nations University Press.

Urata, Shujiro, Yue, Chia Siow and Kimura, Fukunari (eds.) 2006, *Multinationals and economic growth in East Asia: Foreign direct investment, corporate strategies and national economic development*: Routledge.

World Bank 2008, *World Development Report 2009: Reshaping Economic Geographies*: World Bank.

Yusuf, Shahid, Nabeshima, Kaoru and Yamashi, Shoichi (eds.) 2008, *Growing industrial clusters in Asia: Serendipity and Science*: World Bank.

Yin Zhang and Guanghua Wan, 2006, *National Savings and Balanced Growth: China vs. India*: World Bank.

Index

3i Infotech, 105

Aban Offshore Ltd., 134
ABB India, 141
Abu Dhabi, 18, 26, 28, 43, 44, 45, 49, 50, 64, 74, 75, 92, 122, 123, 152, 157
Acer, 96
Adaro Energy, 114
Addax Petroleum Corp., 130, 132
Advanced Heavy Water Reactor, 113
Aeronautical Development Agency, 12
Africa, 1, 2, 7, 79, 131, 132, 133, 134, 142, 162
Agricultural Bank of China, 124, 126
AIG, 120
American Superconductors, 146
Amiad Filtration Systems Ltd., 76
Amtek Auto, 64, 65
Angang Steel, 114
Anta Sports Products Ltd., 58

Apollo Tyres, 65
Aquamundo GmbH, 78
Arab, 16, 23, 44, 91, 92, 93, 123, 153, 156, 157
Arabian Air, 56
Arcelor Mittal, 56
Areva SA, 141, 143, 144
Areva T&D India, 141
ASEAN, 15, 16, 82, 153, 163
Ashok Leyland, 65
Asia Cement, 85
Asia Infrastructure Project Development Private Ltd., 76
Asia Monetary Fund, 46
Asian Development Bank (ADB), 18, 76, 82
Asia-Pacific, 15, 24, 53, 117, 131, 134, 135, 137, 138, 156
Astra Microwave, 111
ASUS, 96
Australia, 7, 78, 112, 113, 115, 131, 132, 135, 146, 156, 166

Awilco Offshore, 134
Axis Bank, 118

Babcock & Wilcox, 144
Bahrain, 16, 153, 156
Baidu.com, 98, 103, 104
Bajaj Auto Ltd., 61, 62, 65
Baker Hughes, 134
Bangladesh, 153
Bank of Canada, 112
Bank of China, 124, 166
Bank Sarasin, 80
Bansal Classes Private Ltd., 36
Baoshan Iron & Steel, 114
Beijing Automotive Industries Holding
    Co. (BAIC), 97
Beijing Capital Company, 57
Belle International, 59
Berlinwasser International
    AG, 75, 79
Bharat Forge Ltd., 64, 145
Bharat Heavy Electricals Ltd. (BHEL),
    83, 141, 145
Bharti Airtel, 101
BHP Billiton, 114
Blackstone Group, 166
Bombardier Inc., 85
Bosch Ltd., 65
BP, 133, 138, 143
BRIC, 16, 17
Bumi Resources, 114, 140
business-process outsourcing
    (BPO), 105
BYD Co., 98, 149

Cable and Satellite Broadcasting
    Association of Asia (CASBAA), 68
Cambodia, 27, 30, 152, 155, 156
Canada, 7, 62, 107, 112, 113, 115,
    121, 130, 133
Changyou.com Ltd., 102, 103
Charoen Pokhpand Foods Ltd., 90
Cheung Kong Holdings, 47

Chevron, 113, 133
Chi Mei Optoelectronics Corp., 106
China, 1, 2, 3, 4, 5, 6, 7, 8, 9, 10, 11,
    12, 13, 14, 15, 16, 17, 18, 19, 20,
    21, 22, 23, 24, 25, 26, 27, 29, 30,
    31, 32, 33, 34, 35, 37, 38, 39, 40,
    41, 43, 44, 45, 47, 48, 51, 52, 53,
    57, 58, 60, 61, 62, 66, 67, 68, 69,
    71, 72, 73, 74, 75, 76, 77, 78, 79,
    80, 81, 82, 83, 84, 85, 86, 87, 88,
    89, 90, 91, 95, 96, 97, 98, 99, 100,
    101, 102, 103, 104, 106, 107, 108,
    109, 110, 112, 113, 114, 115, 118,
    119, 120, 121, 122, 124, 125, 126,
    129, 130, 131, 132, 133, 134, 135,
    137, 138, 139, 140, 141, 142, 143,
    144, 145, 146, 147, 148, 152, 153,
    154, 155, 157, 158, 159, 160, 161,
    162, 163, 164, 165, 166, 179, 180
China CITIC Bank, 124
China Coal, 114
China Construction Bank, 124
China Distance Education Holdings
    Ltd., 39
China Educational Alliance Inc., 40
China Enterprise Company Ltd., 57
China High Speed Transmission
    Equipment Co., 146
China Hydraulic Engineering
    Society, 73
China Investment Corporation (CIC),
    165, 166
Chinalco, 115
China Life, 120, 121
China Minmetals, 115
China Mobile, 96, 100, 101, 104, 107
China Oilfield Services Ltd.
    (COSL), 134
China Overseas Land and Investment
    Ltd. (COLI), 43
China Petroleum and Chemical
    Corporation (Sinopec), 132, 133,
    137, 139

China Railway Construction Corp. (CRCC), 87
China Real Estate Information Corp., 103
China Resources Land, 48
China Shenhua, 114
China Southern Power Grid, 143
China Taiping Insurance Holdings, 120
China TransInfo Technology Corp., 103
China Wind Power International Corporation, 146
China Yangtze Power, 141
Chinese Fine Art Fund, 67
Claymore S&P Global Water Index ETF, 80
CNOOC, 132, 137
coal-bed methane (CBD), 134, 142
Coal India Ltd., 114
Congo, 131
Container Corporation of India, 88
CPN Leasehold Growth, 46
Crayon Capital Fund, 67
Crest Spring Private Ltd., 76
Cyber Jaya City, 47

Daewoo Engineering & Construction, 80
Daewoo Securities, 119
Daewoo Shipbuilding and Marine Engineering Company, 136
Daphne International, 59
Darco Water Technologies Ltd., 77
Datang International Power Generation Company, 141
Datang Telecom, 107, 109
Dayen International, 76
Defense Research and Development Organization (DRDO), 111
Democratic Republic of Congo, 131
Deng Xiaoping, 3
Deutsche Bahn AG, 92
Digitech, 107
direct-to-home TV, 68, 101

DLF, 56
D-Link, 96
Dolphin Offshore, 134
Dongfang Electric Corp., 142
Dongfeng Group, 63
Doosan Heavy Industry, 80, 84
drilling rigs, 134
Dubai Ports World Ltd., 93

East Africa, 1, 2
East Asia, 5, 8, 13, 14, 15, 16, 17, 29, 45, 51, 55, 57, 90, 105, 106, 122, 152, 153, 159, 160, 161, 167
EBITDA, 133
Economic Cooperation Framework Agreement (ECFA), 163
Electrosteel Casting, 80
ELK, 107
emerging Asia, 4, 10, 12, 17, 83, 95, 97, 99, 106, 108, 112, 113, 114, 118, 120, 134, 135, 179
Energy Information Administration (EIA), 113
Ephindo, 143
Europe, 2, 3, 7, 18, 26, 29, 53, 54, 72, 76, 78, 87, 92, 97, 108, 109, 117, 120, 123, 130, 134, 138, 145, 146, 156, 157
European Union, 15, 90, 152
exchange traded funds (ETFs), 80, 81, 125, 126
Exxon Mobil, 133

FAW Car Co., 63
First Ship Lease Trusts (FSLT), 86
foreign direct investment (FDI), 24, 31
free-trade agreements (FTA), 7, 15, 45, 46, 61, 160, 163
Future Advanced Composite Components AG, 111
Future Park Property Fund, 46

Gabon, 131, 133
GAIL India Ltd., 136

Gas Turbine Research Establishment, 12
Gaz de France, 136
Gazprom, 130
GE, 144, 145
Geely Automobile Holdings, 60, 97
GE Hitachi Nuclear Energy Ltd., 145
Genting Malaysia Berhad, 52
Germany, 78, 145
GM, 11, 62, 97, 144, 148
GMR, 144
Great Eastern Energy Corp.
    (GEEC), 144
Great Wall Motors, 63
Green Dragon Gas Ltd., 142
Guangxi Liugong Machinery, 84
Gujarat NRE Coke, 114
Gulf Cooperation Council (GCC),
    16, 17, 23, 24, 28, 44, 50, 71, 79,
    123, 156
Gulf of Mexico, 133

Haier Electronics Group Co. Ltd., 98
Halliburton, 134, 142
Hang Seng China Enterprises Index
    (HSCEI), 4, 125
Harbin Power Equipment Co. Ltd.,
    142, 144
Harvest Energy Trust, 133
Hengdeli Holdings Ltd., 58
Hero Honda Ltd., 61, 62, 65
Hindustan Aeronautics Ltd., 12
Hindustan Construction Co.,
    82, 83, 144
Hong Kong, 4, 8, 16, 21, 29, 41, 43,
    45, 47, 48, 51, 53, 58, 63, 68, 78,
    90, 96, 109, 114, 125, 126, 137,
    153, 161
Housing Development Finance
    Corporation (HDFC), 118
H-shares, 4
Hsinchu, Taiwan, 47
HTC, 96, 107, 109
Huawei, 96, 109

hydro-power, 146
Hyflux Ltd., 76, 78
Hyundai, 97
Hyundai Engineering &
    Construction, 80

ICICI Bank, 67, 118, 121
i-Flex Solutions Ltd., 105
India, 2, 3, 4, 5, 6, 7, 8, 9, 10, 11, 12,
    13, 14, 15, 16, 17, 18, 19, 20, 21,
    22, 23, 24, 25, 26, 27, 31, 32, 34,
    35, 36, 37, 40, 41, 43, 47, 51, 53,
    54, 56, 58, 60, 61, 62, 64, 65, 66,
    67, 68, 71, 72, 73, 76, 78, 79, 80,
    82, 83, 85, 87, 88, 89, 91, 93, 95,
    96, 97, 98, 99, 100, 101, 103, 104,
    105, 106, 107, 108, 109, 110, 111,
    112, 113, 114, 118, 119, 120, 121,
    122, 126, 130, 131, 132, 134, 135,
    136, 137, 138, 139, 140, 141, 142,
    143, 144, 145, 146, 147, 148, 149,
    152, 153, 154, 155, 157, 158, 159,
    160, 161, 162, 164, 165, 167, 180
Indiabulls Properties Investment
    Trust, 56
Indian Fine Art Fund, 67
Indian Hotels Ltd., 54
Indonesia, 5, 7, 12, 19, 24, 27, 30, 31,
    48, 53, 68, 71, 80, 81, 82, 85, 90,
    93, 95, 99, 109, 113, 114, 118, 122,
    132, 135, 136, 140, 141, 143, 152,
    153, 161, 180
Indraprastha Gas Ltd., 137
Industrial and Commercial Bank of
    China (ICBC), 19, 98, 124; 166
Inner Mongolia Baotou Steel
    Rare-Earth Hi-Tech Co., 113
Inner Mongolia Yili Industrial
    Group, 90
Innolux Display Corp., 106
Insituform Technologies Inc., 78
International Monetary Fund (IMF),
    10, 18

Iran, 131, 135, 152, 157, 158
Iraq, 2, 92, 133, 157
Israel, 27, 31, 59, 71, 75, 76, 91,
    105, 109, 152, 155, 157, 158, 161,
    167, 180
IVRCL Infrastructure Ltd., 80, 83

Japan, 4, 7, 8, 9, 11, 14, 15, 16, 17, 18,
    21, 24, 25, 27, 29, 31, 34, 35, 45,
    51, 53, 60, 61, 68, 71, 80, 97, 99,
    100, 101, 104, 107, 109, 113, 115,
    117, 118, 120, 122, 123, 126, 127,
    130, 131, 132, 135, 144, 153, 155,
    158, 159, 160, 161, 162, 164
Japanese Exim Bank, 131
Japan Steel Works (JSW) Ltd., 143
J-COM Co. Ltd., 68
JFE Holdings Inc., 80
Jiangsu Expressway Co. Ltd., 86
Jindal Steel & Power Ltd., 87
Jordan, 91, 157

Kazakhstan, 113
Kazatomprom, 112
KEC International, 141
Khmer Rouge, 156
KIA Motors, 97
Koeningsegg Group AB, 97
Konzen Group, The, 76
Korea Development Bank (KDB), 127
Korea Electric Power, 140
Korea Express, 80
Kubota Corp, 80
Kurdistan, 33
Kurita Water Industries Ltd., 80
Kuwait, 16, 23, 28, 91, 93, 153, 156
Kuwait Chemicals, 91

LaCrosse, 148
Land & Houses Public Co., 54
Larsen & Toubro, 83, 111, 141, 145
Las Vegas Sands Corporation, 52
Latin America, 18, 132

LG Display Co. Ltd., 106
LG Electronics, 108
Libya, 131
LIC Housing Finance, 118
Linguaphone Group Plc, 37
LNG, 115, 132, 136
LNG tankers, 136
LNG terminals, 131, 135
Lonking Holdings Ltd., 84
Lotus Learning, 37
LPG, 137

Magna International, 62
Major Cineplex Lifestyle Lease, 46
Malaysia, 12, 30, 31, 41, 45, 47, 52,
    53, 68, 71, 76, 79, 80, 81, 93, 99,
    113, 131, 136, 153, 161, 180
Malaysian Shipping, 136
Manila Stock Exchange, 147
Mapletree Logistics Trust (MLT), 45
Maruichi Steel Tubes, 80
Maruti Suzuki, 65
McKinsey & Co., 34, 91, 118
Mead Johnson Nutrition, 91
Mediatek Inc., 107
Mengniu Dairy, 90
Metito Overseas, 79
MFC Global Investment
    Management, 126
Middle East, 14, 23, 27, 28, 29, 30,
    31, 49, 50, 51, 55, 57, 64, 67, 79,
    91–93, 131, 132, 138, 139, 152,
    156, 157, 166, 180
Ministry of Trade and Industry,
    Singapore, 76
Mobile Telecommunications Co. Ltd., 93
Molycorp, 113
Morgan Stanley, 166
MSCI Golden Dragon index, 126
Multimedia Super Corridor,
    Malaysia, 47
Mumbai Metro, 85
Myanmar, 151

Nanjing Zhongbei, 85
NASDAQ, 21, 102, 103, 146
National Aerospace Laboratories, 12
National Association of Software
   and Services Companies
   (NASSCOM), 103
National Iranian Oil Company, 131
National Oil Co., 132, 133, 147
natural gas, 24, 91, 92, 130, 132, 134,
   135, 136, 137
NCSoft Corporation, 101
Neowiz Games, 101
Netafim Ltd., 91
Netease.com, Inc., 102, 103
New Hope Agribusiness Co. Ltd.
   (NHA), 89, 90
New Oriental Education
   Technology, 38
NHN Corp., 103
NIFTY Index, 4, 9
Nigeria, 131, 133,
North Korea, 158
North West Shelf Venture, 131
Norway, 87, 134
Nuclear Power Corporation
   (NPC), 144
NYSE, 21, 39, 74

oil and gas, 26, 27, 111, 131, 132,
   133, 136
Oman, 16, 48, 153, 157
ONGC, 132, 136
Osian Art Fund, 67

Pacific Shipping Trust (PST), 86
Pakistan, 146, 153, 158
Patel Engineering, 83
Pearl River Delta, 47
Pearson Plc, 12, 38
People's Insurance Company of
   China (PICC), 120
Persian Gulf, 92, 99, 152
Peru, 133

PetroChina, 130, 132, 137, 139, 143
Petronet LNG, 136
Philippine National Oil
   Corporation, 147
Philippines, 27, 31, 48, 53, 68, 69, 71,
   81, 90, 139, 147, 152, 153
Ping An, 120
PixArt, 107
PNOC Energy Development
   Corporation (EDC), 147
Political Instability Index, 153
Poly Real Estate Group, 57
Ports Design Ltd., 58, 59
POSCO, 114
Power Grid Corporation of India, 143
PowerShares Water Resources Portfolio
   ETF, 81
Prudential, 121
PT Holcim Indonesia, 85
PT Indocement, 85
PTT Exploration & Production, 132

Qatar, 16, 23, 50, 92, 135, 136, 153
Qatar Gas Transport Company, 36
Quality Property Houses Fund, 46

Raimon Land Co., 55
Real Estate Investment Trusts (REITs),
   45, 46, 56
Red Chips, 4
refineries, 24, 113, 131, 137, 138,
   139, 142
Reliance Communications, 7, 101
Reliance Infrastructure, 85, 141
Reliance Power, 144
REpower AG, 146
Rhodia, 113
Rickmers Maritime (RMT), 86
Rio Tinto, 114, 115
Rosneft, 130, 134
Royal Dutch Shell, 133
Russia, 16, 22, 55, 130, 131, 133, 134,
   144, 145, 162

S&P 500, 4
SABIC, 91
SAIC Motor Corp., 148
Salcon Berhad, 79
Samsung Fire & Marine Insurance, 119
Samsung Heavy Industries, 136
Samui Airport Property Fund, 46
Sands Macau Ltd., 52
Sansiri, 54
Sany Heavy Equipment, 114
Sarasin Sustainable Water Fund, 80
Saudi Arabia, 6, 23, 29, 50, 74, 79, 92, 122, 153, 156, 157, 158
Saudi Arabian Amiantit Company, 78
Saudi Arabian Fertilizer Company (SAFCO), 91
Saudi Telecom, 93
Schlumberger, 134
Securities and Exchange Board of India, 66
Sembcorp Marine, 134
Sesa Goa, 114
Shanda Games Ltd., 102
Shanghai Electric Group Co. Ltd., 142
Shanghai Property Index, 44
Shenzhen Stock Exchange, 85
shipyards, 86, 87, 136
Sichuan Tengzhong Heavy Industrial Machinery, 97
Siemens India, 141
Singapore, 8, 14, 16, 17, 18, 21, 29, 43, 45, 46, 52, 53, 55, 56, 76, 77, 78, 84, 86, 117, 123, 134, 153, 161, 166
S-Oil Corp., 138
South America, 131
South Asia, 152, 155
South East Asia, 53
South Korea, 8, 11, 14, 16, 18, 29, 40, 45, 46, 48, 51, 53, 60, 71, 80, 82, 95, 99, 101, 106, 119, 120, 123, 138, 143, 153, 155, 157, 158, 160, 161

Spain, 145
Sri Lanka, 2, 158
Ssangyong Motors, 97
State Bank of India, 118
State Grid Corp., 143
Stock Exchange of Thailand, 46, 90
STX Group, 86
Sudan, 131
Suez Environment, 74, 75, 81
Sumitomo Corp., 113
Sumitomo Heavy Industries, 80
Sun Hang Kai Development, 47–48
super-majors, 132
Suzlon Energy, 40, 146
Suzuki Motors, 62
Syria, 133, 157

Taiwan, 14, 16, 21, 22, 25, 27, 29, 30, 41, 47, 51, 58, 71, 82, 95, 96, 99, 103, 106, 107, 109, 120, 126, 135, 153, 154, 155, 160, 161, 163, 180
Taiwan Semiconductor Manufacturing Company, 25
Tanganyika Oil Company, 133
Tata Motors, 60, 62, 65, 82, 97, 149
Tata Nano, 148
Tata Power, 144
Tata Steel, 114
Teck Cominco, 115
Teekay LNG, 136
Tencent Holdings, 102
Thailand, 14, 46, 48, 53, 54, 55, 60, 68, 80, 81, 90, 118, 132, 151, 152, 153
Thai President Foods Ltd., 90
Thames Water Plc, 74
Thermax Ltd., 80
Three Gorges Dam, 141
Tianjin FAW Xiali Auto, 63
TOPIX, 4
Toronto Stock Exchange, 130
Tourism Development and Investment Company (TDIC), 49, 50

Toyota Motors, 113
Transocean, 134
TrendMicro, 96
Tsingtao Breweries, 68
Turkey, 87

Ultra-Flo Pte. Ltd., 76
UN, 156
Unitech, 56
United Arab Emirates (UAE), 16, 23, 44, 49, 50, 153, 156, 157
United Engineers Singapore, 76
United Nations Economic and Social Commission for Asia and the Pacific (UNESCAP), 42, 43
United Overseas Bank, 117
United States (US), 3, 6, 7, 8, 9, 10, 11, 14, 15, 17, 27, 29, 34, 40, 52, 54, 57, 60, 76, 79, 97, 98, 107, 109, 110, 113, 115, 118, 120, 121, 123, 127, 130, 131, 138, 142, 144, 145, 146, 148, 156, 157, 159, 160, 162, 163, 164
UN Population Fund, 73
US Department of Energy, 113, 134
Uzbekistan, 133

Vajpayee, Atal Behari, 22
Vanke, 47, 98
Vedanta Plc, 114
Veolia Environment, 74, 75, 81, 85, 147
Veolia Transport, 85
Veolia Water, 74
Vietnam, 5, 7, 11, 12, 31, 32, 61, 68, 71, 80, 90, 95, 101, 109, 113, 131, 153, 158, 180

Wall Street Institute, 38
Walt Disney Company, The, 37

Weatherford, 134
Weichai Power Equipment, 63
Wen Jiabao, 164
Western Australia, 131, 132
Westinghouse Electric Co., 143, 144, 145
wind-power, 145, 146
wind-turbine, 113, 142, 146
Wipro Technologies, 7, 105
Woodside Petroleum Ltd. (WPL), 115
World Tourism Organization (UNWTO), 50, 51
World Travel and Tourism Council, 53
WPP Group Plc, 99
WTO, 14, 23, 119, 154
Wuhan Iron and Steel Corp., 114
Wumart, 59

XinAo Gas, 137
Xinjiang Goldwind Science & Technology Company, 146
Xi'an Aircraft Industry Group, 111

Yakult Honsha Co. Ltd., 91
Yantai Changyu Pioneer Wine Company, 96
Yatra Capital, 56
Yaxley Consulting, 40
Yemen Arab Republic, 92
Yuanta Financial Holding Co., 120
Yue Yuen Industrial Holdings Ltd., 109

Zee Entertainment, 68
Zee News Ltd., 68
Zhejiang Expressway Co. Ltd., 86
Zheng He, 1
ZTE Corporation, 106, 107, 109